NOW THIS

NOW

THIS

G. P. PUTNAM'S SONS
NEW YORK

Radio,

Television...

and the

Real World

J U D Y

M U L L E R

G. P. Putnam's Sons
Publishers Since 1838
a member of
Penguin Putnam Inc.
375 Hudson Street
New York, NY 10014

Library of Congress Cataloging-in-Publication Data

Muller, Judy.
Now this : radio, television . . . and the real world / by Judy Muller.
p.   cm.
ISBN 0-399-14619-9
1. Muller, Judy.   2. Television journalists—United States—Biography.
I. Title
PN4874.M794   A3   2000   99-087257
070'.92—dc21
[B]

Printed in the United States of America
1   3   5   7   9   10   8   6   4   2

This book is printed on acid-free paper. ∞

Book design by Lynne Amft

Acknowledgments

I want to thank my dad, Jack Mansfield, for his constant encouragement and for reminding me, in those moments when I didn't believe I could do it, that I could. More important, I thank him for all the stories: the ones told by the campfire, the ones told at bedtime and at bad times, the ones he told to my kids, who will no doubt tell their kids, the ones that helped me know just how to start this book.

And grudging thanks to my brother, Johnny, whose ceaseless teasing over the years has helped hone my sense of the absurd and teach me never to take anything too seriously, especially myself.

This book would never have been written without a healthy shove from my friends Eric and Maureen Lasher, who also happen to be literary agents. They patiently shopped my book proposal around, despite a number of "Judy *who?*" responses, until a few publishers actually expressed interest, including one who wanted only those stories in the proposal that centered on flyfishing and one who wanted only those stories that never, ever mentioned flyfishing. Being the literary whore that I am, I quickly agreed to do either, depending on who would pay the most. I guess flyfishing will have to wait for the next book.

Neil Nyren, my editor at Putnam, may not be a fan of fly-fishing, but HE has a fan in me. He managed to take someone who had never written anything other than a short news piece and turn her into someone who could write a short book. But a book, nonetheless! He did this, mostly, by believing in me right from the start and encouraging me every step of the way. As someone who works in network news, I found this a refreshing concept.

I also want to thank all my friends at the ABC News Bureau in Los Angeles who have listened to me agonize about this venture all year long but who have, through all the whining, cheered me on. Especially Beth, Laura, and Dawn, who provided invaluable feedback.

I also want to thank Harriet Wrye, my tour guide to the truth, who kept me honest when glib would have been easier, and my pal Leslie Fuller for her wit and wisdom and love, and the Women of Friday Night for All Of The Above.

And many, many, many thanks to Kristen and Kerry, without whom this book would not be possible. And don't worry, kids. From now on, everything is off the record. Really.

For Kristen and Kerry

Contents

NOW THIS

CHAPTER

1

LIVING
TO TELL
THE STORY

Without art, the crudeness of reality
would make life unbearable.

— GEORGE BERNARD SHAW

I come from a family of storytellers, to whom I owe my occasional forays into sanity. No matter how miserable the moment, whether it's just a bad blind date or a devastating
custody battle, there is a small storyteller in my brain who pulls
up a chair, whips out a notebook, and starts jotting down each
gory detail, all the while whispering, "Hey, at least it will make
a *great story!*"

The Buddhists might call this "Mindfulness," but in my case,
I suspect it has more to do with survival than serenity. As long as
that reporter-in-residence is scribbling away, angst is eventually
edited into anecdote, that invaluable refuge from reality that can
turn agony into acceptance, horror into humor. Especially
humor—the sort that delivers an electric charge of irony to the
brain, rendering self-pity just about impossible to sustain for any
period of time, no matter how finely honed your wallowing
skills might be.

While this talent for observing absurdity might be satisfying
on a personal level, not to mention fairly profitable on a professional level, it can also be a burden. Let's face it, seeing the per-

verse and the ironic in situations does not always endear you to others.

This was driven home to me on my very first job in journalism. While on maternity leave from teaching high school English in suburban New Jersey, I decided to try my hand at writing a column for a small newspaper, the sort of paper that gets tossed on your lawn every week whether you want it or not, meaning the free kind, used primarily to line bird cages. The kind of newspaper where, I figured, a budding columnist could wield irony with impunity (that is to say almost anonymously, since the words would soon be covered by parakeet poop anyway).

At least, that's what I thought. But the very first column I submitted also gave me my very first lesson in the power of the press, no matter how puny. It was a satirical piece about the latest keeping-up-with-the-Joneses mania that had taken hold of my suburban community, in which folks had been swept up in a competitive compulsion to wallpaper every crevice in the house. I mean, it was not an exaggeration to suggest that basement crawl spaces in my neighborhood were bedecked in flock and foil. Okay, it *was* an exaggeration, but irony sometimes requires it. This piece, written in Erma-Noir style (as in Bombeck, but much, much darker), got an instant reaction from the managing editor of said puny paper. "This is *hilarious*," she said on the phone. "It's convulsed everyone in the office (meaning her and the advertising salesman). But are you *sure* you want us to run this?"

"Why *not?*" I wondered. I soon found out. At the next neighborhood barbecue, I was introduced to the ancient tradition of shunning. Oh sure, a few brave souls spoke, but usually to furtively ask something along the lines of: "That wasn't *me* you were talking about with the grass cloth in the laundry room, was it?" "Oh *no*," I'd lie, even as I wondered who the hell *else* had thought to wallpaper the laundry tub.

But shunning would be the downside. Arguably a pretty *big* downside in that case, considering the twenty-five-dollar-a-column remuneration. No, it's the upside that keeps the hardcore storyteller coming back for more. Because when kindred souls do connect over a good story, the result can be life-saving. "Oh, thank God," you think, "someone else gets it. I'm not alone, after all."

As I said, I consider this mixed blessing something of a family legacy, one that began, near as I can tell, with my father's father, who would keep us grandchildren spellbound with the adventures of a daring little boy who outwitted lurking predators, from desperados to cougars, in the Blue Mountains near our hometown in eastern Oregon.

These were magical mountains to me, populated by tall tamaracks, lush ferns, deep carpets of moss, meadows of wild strawberries, and, in the summertime, most of my relatives, who used to escape the heat of the valley by fleeing to their family cabins. The Blue Mountains unfold gradually out of the wheat fields surrounding another place of almost mythical importance in my mind, the town of Milton-Freewater (the hyphen a symbol of stubborn pride between two very small towns that agreed to merge only if they could hold on to their admittedly obscure identities). If you should ever happen to drive through it, you would not understand this, of course. You'd probably see a bunch of bars and a bunch of churches, a few shuttered stores that have seen better times, a few grain elevators—you know, the usual stuff of small towns you drive through and never think about again. That is, if you ever thought about it *while* you were driving through.

But if you were a little girl whose father's Navy career meant moving every two or three years, you would see Milton-Freewater as a hyphenated heaven, the one place that could undeniably be called "home," a place where one grandfather held the lofty position of manager of the Stadelman Fruit Packing Plant, and the other managed the Tum-A-Lum Lumber Company, a Wobegonish name, to be sure, but true. Years later, when I first heard the term "aromatherapy," I assumed it must be connected to the soothing smells of childhood, which for me would have included the aroma given off from the hardwood floors of that packing plant after it had absorbed years and years of ripe cherries, aromatic apples, and parfum des prunes. Add a scintilla of sawdust and we're talking nasal nirvana. So far, I haven't found these scents in a bottle; a true fix requires an occasional visit to a general store or fruit stand with hardwood floors. And, of course, a sawmill.

The fruit-packing granddad, Barlow Clark, was not a garrulous guy, but rather a master of brevity and understatement, valuable skills for any storyteller. He would normally speak up only if directly questioned about something, such as the time we asked him about a funeral he'd just attended for one of his cousins.

"Yep, we lost a good man there. 'Course, he had some rough years at the end."

"Oh? And why's that?"

"Well, he was doing fine, working as town sheriff and all, and then his wife up and disappeared."

"That's terrible. Did they ever find her?"

"Yep. The rumors just got too numerous to ignore."

"Rumors?"

"The rumors about the new floor at the jail."

"No."

"Yep. He put that floor in right about the time she disappeared. 'Course, the two of 'em never did get along. Fact is, *no* one liked her. Awful woman."

"So what happened?"

"Well, darlin' " (this affectionate term always signalled a wrap-up), "they dug up the floor and found the body and he went to jail, that's what happened." (Long pause, sigh). "Damn shame, too."

"Why's that, Barlow?"

"He was the best damned sheriff this town ever had."

When it came to pure skills of description, however, it was my father's father, the lumberman, who was so limber with a story. The tale I remember most vividly, the one that prowled through my childhood dreams, involved a cougar. Our young hero was carefully making his way down a winding mountain trail, after the sun had set, when the horse he was riding was suddenly spooked by the shrill scream of a cougar (in these stories, cougars always "scream like a wild woman"). Thrown from his horse, our plucky lad was forced to wrestle the ferocious cat, and through a combination of wit and daring, lived to tell the story. A story with so much realistic detail that I always assumed the little boy was, in fact, my grandfather, an impression reinforced by his dramatic gesturing with a hand that was missing a few fingers. Years later, I learned that he had actually lost those fingers while trying to clear a clogged reaper, but it never changed the power of the story, one that left a nagging question in our impressionable young minds. To wit, would *we* have the wit to survive a similar encounter, face to face with a wild animal on a dark trail, and would *we* live to tell the story?

My Dad picked up where his father left off, telling tales (actually based on facts!) of a family of lowlifes known as, well, let's just call them the Skaggit Brothers, who ran a lumber mill in those same mountains in the twenties and thirties. They would hire poor laborers in town, work them nearly to death with little food or water, pay them a week's wages, then don masks and rob their own employees on the trail back to town. Those who resisted were shot on the spot. It was said their bodies were buried in a mountainous sawdust pile next to the Skaggit Mill.

Word of these less-than-ideal working conditions eventually got around, of course, forcing the Skaggit Boys to go farther and farther afield to find workers. "Farther even than Walla Walla?" we'd ask. Although Walla Walla was not that far away in miles, it *was* in a different state and, during daylight savings, in a different time zone as well, so it had an exotic ring, phonetically and geographically. "You bet," said Dad, "as far as Portland and Boise!"

This story had many variations, but its impact was strongest when told at night around a campfire not far from the deserted mill featured in the story. Sometimes we would venture near that sarcophagus of sawdust, but only in daylight hours. It never occurred to us to question the truth of the story, or to wonder why the authorities had never actually searched for bodies there. I suppose that, even then, we must have known that some stories are just better left alone. Besides, every kid should have a sawdust pile or a cougar in his family mythology, a place where evil things lurk, a predator to test our nerve. Scary metaphors can be very useful, even years later.

Like anybody else who's lived long enough to tell a story or two, I've encountered my share of cougars and Skaggits along the way. And like anybody else who makes a living telling stories, I've come to see these encounters as, essentially, great material, much to the dismay of my kids, who learned very early to preface their most quotable remarks with, "Mom, this *has* to be off the record."

As a correspondent for ABC News and a commentator for NPR's *Morning Edition,* I have had limitless opportunities to hear, and tell, some fascinating stories, from presidential campaigns to earthquakes to O. J. Simpson. But let's face it (I certainly have), there are much more celebrated reporters out there who have done the same. So this book is not about the Big "Get," as our increasingly tabloidized profession refers to such major scoops as uncovering a candidate's peccadillos (a marvelous example of onomatopoeia, if there ever was one).

No, it's about the "Little Get" or, shall we say, the Get-a-load-of-*This,*" culled from a lifetime of behind-the-scenes observations scribbled down by that reporter in the brain who feels compelled to bear witness to the ironic and perverse. And by "behind-the-scenes," I mean a gamut of experiences picked up along the way, the "way" including radio reporting for local stations in Princeton and Denver, and then for the CBS Radio Network in New York, much of the time while trying to raise two young daughters as a single mother; a morning-drive commentary for CBS News called *First Line Report,* which examined major issues in the news each day, often interwoven with personal observations (hence our ubiquitous household phrase of "no comment"); and in my mid-forties, long after any sane person would consider starting a television career, a whole new episode of my life with ABC News, including *World News Tonight, 20/20, Good Morning America, Nightline*—the whole enchilada, as they say in California, which was where my daughters and I suddenly found ourselves.

But all that biography is mere topography. Under the surface burble the sorts of experiences which, when allowed to percolate up, might strike an empathic chord or, more important, an empathic chuckle. There are plenty of stories here about the strange and wondrous world of electronic journalism, to be sure, but there are just as many about that perilous intersection between single parenthood and a broadcasting career, where deadlines and daughters collide on a regular basis—experiences which, taken singly, might seem like no more than irritating grains of sand, but which would, over time, transform a timid pushover into a tough pearl. Or, if a man were doing the describing, a tough broad. Or, as I would be called in later years, "difficult." To this day, I have never heard a male reporter described as "difficult." "Aggressive," perhaps. "Tough." But never "difficult." But I'm getting ahead of myself.

We're not talking here about huge stones in the road. We're talking pebbles, for the most part, those little guys that trip you up simply because you can't see them coming. Parodoxically petty but perilous pebbles that, yes, prompt shameless alliteration but also, with any luck, a jolt of insight. These moments almost always occur just when you think you've got it made, when you've reached a place where "petty" can't possibly hurt you, a place called pride (which would, I think, make a great title for a country tune), and we all know what that goeth before.

Like the time, smack dab in the middle of my upwardly mo-bile, pretty-damn-sure-of-myself career in network radio, when my boss at CBS called me in to suggest that I work on the way I was saying "Now this," just before a commercial break. This def-initely qualified as a pebble. And it was all the more memorable because it took aim at possibly the only thing I was secure about: my on-air delivery.

"How many ways can you say it?" I thought to myself, but dutifully practiced different inflections—NOWTHIS! (authori-tative), nooowwwwww thisssss (provocative), now, this? (inquis-itive)—until I had it just right. Which is basically the way I was saying it before, but with a touch of suspense: now (pregnant pause) this.

It was an interesting exercise, this now-this nonsense, a lesson in understanding that, just when you think you've got a thing wired, something comes along to short-circuit that notion, to pull you up short and remind you that *now*, of all things, you must deal with *this*. It may be something petty, or improbable, or un-predictable, but you cannot proceed without dealing with it. Now this, indeed. As a mantra for dealing with those annoying stones in the Road to Difficult, "now this" works as well as any-thing.

CHAPTER

2

—————

RADIO DAYS

—————

There is a basic principle that distinguishes
a hot medium like radio from a cool one . . .
Hot media are . . . low in participation,
and cool media are high in participation
or completion by the audience.

—Marshall McLuhan

I would like to take this opportunity to apologize to hundreds of my former high-school English students who lost two or three weeks of their lives in a forced march through the tangled thickets of Marshall McLuhan's global village, led only by my dubious tracking skills. What can I say? I was young, the book *The Medium Is the Message* was considered cutting edge, it seemed the right thing to do at the time. In retrospect, now that I have been massaged by the message up close and professional, I can at last confess: I have no idea what the man was talking about.

Take the above quote, for example. Radio, he says, is a hot medium, requiring no participation from the audience, while television is a cool medium, which calls on the audience to fill in the blanks. Quite frankly, it seems just the opposite to me. Tune in to *This American Life,* hosted by public radio's Ira Glass, and its masterful storytelling will prompt you to set the scene, flesh out the characters, change the camera angles, all in your head. Now tune in to *Dateline* or *20/20*. You will be held hostage to every special effect modern TV technology can muster, including slow-motion, computer graphics, maudlin music, mood lighting, and filters that take at least ten years off the faces of anchors, rendering them strangely ephemeral and otherworldly. I, for one, would never vote to remove such age-defying filters from the TV bag of tricks, at least not as long as I'm one of the tricksters. I mention them only to make the point that, on radio, they are superfluous. The listener is in charge of special effects, and that includes conjuring up a face to go with the voice.

Sometimes listeners are disappointed if they happen to encounter the actual bodies that house their favorite radio voices. When I was on CBS radio, for example, people were always expressing their surprise that I was not as tall or as imposing as they had imagined, which was, let's face it, a kind way of saying "My *God,* I never dreamed you'd be so short and ordinary!" When I first met Mike Wallace, he looked at me somewhat askance and said, "*You're* the woman with the balls in her voice?" I think this was a compliment, but it also reflected the prejudice of the times: To have any credibility, a woman delivering the news on radio had to sound like a man.

Even so, I have always loved radio for its intimacy and clarity. It is the one medium where the choice of words is still considered paramount, and the way those words are delivered is still considered an art. If you want proof of the difference, just listen to any television news report with your eyes closed. The words rarely soar, unless you are talking about words written by someone like Jim Wooten of ABC or the late Charles Kuralt of CBS (yes, there are others, and you know who you are, so don't hold it against me). Too often, the words are pedestrian creatures, hitching a ride on the pictures, delivered by a voice that is either forgettable or regrettable.

The fact that my vocal chords have the timbre of authority is not exactly a talent I can claim as hard-earned; it's clearly the luck of the genetic draw, much as really gorgeous people have the edge in television. That's one reason I will always keep a toe in the so-called "hot" medium of radio: My voice, I figure, will be the *last* thing to go.

My radio career began after I had quit my teaching job in New Jersey to be home with my two baby daughters. Having spotted the limitations of writing for the aforementioned weekly newspaper (namely, no money and no hope of any), I decided to try my hand, and voice, at radio news.

I applied for a job at a little station, WHTG in Eatontown, owned by a family that had set up a studio in an old clapboard house. By "little," I mean the kind of place where you were expected to unlock the door in the morning, read all the dials and gauges and radio thingamajigs and note those readings in a log (a skill for which I had been forced to earn a third-class radio license and for which I have no memory whatsoever), turn on the other thingamajigs that got that station actually operational, sit down, switch on the microphone, and start talking. This job paid only slightly more than the newspaper, but I looked at it as on-the-job training. Or I *would* have looked at it that way had I ever actually entered the front door of the place. Two days before I was to start, the news director (who was also the general manager, program director, and sales guy) called to tell me the owners had changed their minds.

"*Why?*" I asked in a crushed voice.

"To tell you the truth," he said, "they're worried that a woman with two small children might be unreliable."

Today, those would be fighting words. Litigious, even. Which is to say that, today, no one would say them out loud. They would merely *think* them, come up with some other excuse, and do the very same thing. But back then, before sexism went underground, employers said outrageous things like that all the time— and women put up with it all the time. Until, that is, they would eventually have enough, and then they would fight back in some way that stopped just short of litigation. For me, WHTG in Eatontown was the first ambush along the trail, the first pounce of the cougar, albeit a minor skirmish.

I had more luck with WHWH in Princeton, a station owned by a man named Herbert W. Hobler (hence the call letters) who had a Dickensian air about him (his idea one year for a Christmas bonus was to offer us all raffle tickets in a drawing for a single turkey), but who also had a fairly expansive vision when it came to radio news. He put together an astonishingly large news staff for such a small station, four or five reporters who did much more than "rip and read" copy off the wires, reporters who covered state politics and local council meetings and board of education meetings and who regularly won awards for their investigative series.

It was my good fortune to wander into this station at a time when broadcasters were under growing pressure to add women to the mix. So, while I had never worked in radio news before, the fact that I could write coherently and speak clearly (and Hey! She sounds like a guy!) pretty much guaranteed me the job. They didn't even care that I could only work part time because of my kids; they were that desperate. This initial job in broadcasting has slanted my thinking on Affirmative Action ever since. While I believe people should be evaluated on the basis of their abilities (which is about as controversial a stand as hoping for peace on earth, and just about as probable), I know I would never have had the chance to demonstrate my own abilities had those men not felt the pressure to add "diversity" long before "diversity" had become the ubiquitous code word for "We need a broad (black/latino/Asian) *now!*"

The news director at this station was a salty statehouse reporter named Bill Schirmann. He encouraged his reporters to dig beneath the tweedy veneer of Princeton politics, to ask tough questions in the oh-so-very-polite atmosphere of that Ivy-League community. And what I learned from that experience I carry with me to this day: There are stories, good stories, in the most unlikely places. They may not be scandalous. They may not be sexy. But they are there for the picking, and if you know how to package them, they can be delicious.

One of the most memorable features I wrote for that station came from a meeting of the town's Shade Tree Commission. I had wandered in by accident, looking for some meeting that was much more compelling (of course, I now forget what) and found this small group of people who met once a month to decide the fate of trees stricken with Dutch Elm Disease or sidewalks buckling from hundred-year-old roots and other such weighty matters. It would have been easy to be snide and whip off a satirical piece about Princetonians who had nothing better to do. But instead, as I listened, I was struck by the sincerity of ordinary folks who volunteer their time to take care of things the rest of us take for granted: healthy trees overhead, nonlethal sidewalks underfoot. And the piece became, instead, a sort of paean to unsung heroes. This is the sort of thing Kuralt did all the time, of course, on a much more sophisticated scale, and which so few broadcasters seem to do anymore. With so many shady characters dominating the news, from O. J. to Monica, I wish we could find room for a few more of the shade-tree variety.

Radio reporting, at this most local of levels, is terrific training in the art of storytelling. You learn to ask good questions (which is to say, the questions that seem too dumb to ask until you see every reporter in the room scribbling down the answer) and to write fast and succinctly. And it teaches you to ad lib. I was assigned to report live from a New Jersey hotel ballroom where Bill Bradley was to give his victory speech after winning a Senate primary election. The room was so noisy I couldn't really hear the cue in my ear to start speaking, but my engineer managed to yell, "Go!" And so I started to talk. And talk. And talk. Problem was, Bradley was late and I had no idea when he would actually walk in the room. Since I had no way of hearing two-way communications with the anchor back at the station, I kept vamping for the next half hour. When I had described the issues, the vote, and the candidate, I went on to describe the people in the room, and then the room itself. (Tip to journalism students: If you can describe the so-called "ballroom" of a Holiday Inn for five minutes, without faltering, you can describe anything.) I was about to start describing the food when Bradley's people announced it would be another half hour before his appearance. So I signed off. I later learned that the station had cut out on me after about ten minutes, but then returned every now and then to see if I was still talking, sort of like joining a program in progress.

"It was amazing," said my news director. "A *tour de force*. We were taking bets to see how long you could last. In fact," he added, "Bradley's speech was sort of anticlimactic. He was so boring, we were taking bets on how long *we* could last."

When my husband was transferred to Denver in 1978, I made

the rounds of the top radio stations there and landed a job at KHOW as a morning news anchor for a pair of comedic disc jockeys named Hal and Charley. It still amazes me that serious journalists ever manage to emerge from these odd-couple beginnings. By "serious," I mean reporters who refer to their pals as "colleagues" and to long, liquid lunches as "meeting with a source." At any rate, reporting the day's events on a morning show where *you* are regularly referred to as "Newsette" makes it tough to maintain your credibility. Not to mention a straight face.

A typical handoff from DJ to Newsette (anxiously awaiting her ever-changing and increasingly bizarre cue) tended to go something like this:

Charley: "Well, Hal, enough of these double entendres about the Bronco cheerleaders and their pompoms. Let's hear what Newsette has for us this morning."

Me: "Three dead in avalanche near Aspen! I'm Judy Muller, in the KHOW newsroom."

If the audience was ever startled by these abrupt segues from fiasco to fact, no one ever complained. Perhaps we'd already become so used to the "happy talk" of television news anchors that the seamless slipping between humor and horror had become routine, even unremarkable. But whatever the challenges of working in tandem with a comedy team, the redeeming aspect of this job was that I had managed to find another radio newsroom that believed in getting reporters out in the field for original investigative work. I remember thinking I had finally "arrived" the day I was honored with an award from the American Bar Association and was served with papers from a law firm informing me I was being sued—both for the same story. The disharmonic convergence of these two events, sweetened by the fact that we went on to win the lawsuit, might be what prompted my knee-jerk response, many years later, when my young journalist daughter nervously called to tell me she'd been named in a lawsuit connected with a story she had worked on for *60 Minutes II.* "Congratulations!" I whooped. "Your first lawsuit!"

KHOW in Denver was also a great place to hone my police beat skills. Part of the job required making early morning calls to various law enforcement types to find out if anything had happened overnight, conversations that introduced me to the oxymoronic world of the police "public information officer," or PIO.

Me: "So, officer, anything exciting to report from the overnight logs?"

PIO: "Well, we found a body on the side of I-70. It was cut up, inside a box, all tied up like a neat package."

Me: "Any suspects in that homicide?"

PIO: "I'm not authorized to say it was a homicide."

Me: "Um, pretty creative suicide, don't you think?"

PIO: "I am not at liberty to speculate. It's under investigation."

Like many local stations then and now, KHOW loved crime stories. I particularly remember a story involving a man police had dubbed "Cut-'em-up-Lou," suspected of murdering his roommate and disposing of the body all over town. Our news director told us that we were to break into programming with a bulletin every time another body part turned up somewhere. Fortunately, there were not enough body parts to give the story legs, as it were, so we never got to the point where we developed a promo along the lines of, "When a body's cut up, we cut in," or something equally offensive. I exaggerate only slightly. When it came to crime stories, this news director had few constraints. I always sensed that he was, in fact, a frustrated cop. The reporters drove company cars emblazoned with the station call letters and equipped with police scanners and two-way radios. We were instructed to sign off our reports from the field with, "This is Judy Muller, KHOW NEWS, reporting from mobile unit twelve, on the move in Downtown Denver." This was quite a mouthful to remember, much less utter, especially when you were actually *on* the move, driving through rush-hour traffic and trying to report live at the same time.

This same guy was also convinced that other stations were monitoring our two-way radio transmissions, so he developed a secret code. When we wanted to tell each other something confidential, we were instructed to say, "Go to channel four," which was apparently a secure line. One new reporter failed to get the memo. When told to "Go to channel four," he simply disappeared. An hour later, someone called our newsroom and asked, "Care to tell us why your guy is sitting out in our parking lot?" It was the TV news director from Channel Four.

When I later learned that this same reporter had been hired at a much higher salary than I was getting (information passed on to me by the irate sisterhood of secretaries in the front office), I stormed into the news director's office to demand why a newcomer would be making more than the morning drive anchor.

"Well," he said, without the slightest twinge of guilt, "because he has a family to support. Your husband makes a good living."

I was stunned. Even in radio, that great temple to testosterone, this was unusually blunt in its sexist overtones, undertones, and every other kind of tone. It was, for me, yet another grain of sand on the way to pearldom, another stone in the road to "difficult."

"If I were to bring in my lawyer tomorrow, would you repeat that?" I asked.

I didn't have a lawyer, of course. But the bluff worked. My salary was made commensurate with the new guy's almost immediately. Which is to say, it finally topped $20,000.

It wasn't enough, or course, to support two children after my divorce in 1981, which was a blessing, in a way. There's something about counting out a handful of cents-off coupons at the supermarket while annoyed shoppers are lined up behind you, or calculating just how long bald tires might last before sending you and your children to a gruesome death off a mountain road, that acts as a powerful motivating force for increasing one's earning power.

First, I looked around for a better job in Denver. A now-defunct station, KWBZ, hired me as a talk radio host, middays, just before a time slot occupied by the controversial and legendary Alan Berg, who later served as the model for the movie *Talk Radio*. Unfortunately, years of conditioning by a mother who drilled me with, "If you can't say anything nice, don't say anything at all" did not make me a terrific candidate for provocative talk radio. I found it almost impossible to cut people off. Hanging up on them was completely out of the question. So I listened, as callers would drone on and on about whatever was bothering them. And since talk radio does not always attract the highest-functioning folk, especially in the middle of the day, my show was chock full of conspiracy theorists who were not taking their medication and lonely shut-ins who were (and how could I hang up on *them?*).

I remember Alan Berg kindly counseling me that I might have to spice up the exchanges just a tad: "You're a cream puff and you need to be a hot tamale." As it turned out, I never really got a chance to sharpen my tongue. I was, instead, struck dumb when the owner of the station called us all one morning to announce that he had filed for bankruptcy and was closing down his whole operation. Four talk show hosts were suddenly scrambling for jobs in a town that really didn't have room for that many hot tamales, never mind a cream puff.

I'd been ambushed by the Skaggit Brothers, and I was ready for the sawdust pile.

I'd like to say I marshaled my mental defenses and fought back, eluding the desperados of depression. But my reaction was to crawl under the covers and cry. I knew I had to find work, but I couldn't seem to muster the will or the energy. It was as though a heavy blanket had been dropped over me, and I couldn't find the edge of it and even if I had found the edge of it, would not have had the strength to pull it off me. I knew this feeling wasn't natural, but instead of recognizing it as depression, I chose to judge it as self-pity, which added even more weight to my self-loathing lethargy.

But while I didn't get the therapy I no doubt could have used (and could never have afforded), I did get enough of a boost to jump-start me toward action. It was an emotional jolt, and it came from my kids. Each morning, in that moment between first consciousness and the first hit of hopelessness, I would sense two small bodies over me, whispering to one another.

"Is she awake yet?"

"I don't know. But we have to wake her up."

"You do it."

"No, you."

And they would. "You have to get up now, Mommy," the eight-year-old would say. "Yeah, Mommy," chimed in her younger sister. "You've got to look for a job."

I'd open my eyes and look into their eyes, and see their fear. And their fear would trump my self-pity. And *my* fear. And so I'd crawl out from under my dis-comforter, get up from my mattress on the floor in my domicile of divorce—the ironically named Happy Canyon Condominiums—go out to the harvest gold and avocado green kitchen, throw together breakfast from the generic brands du jour, drive them to school on treacherous tires, and start making the rounds of radio stations. It was exhausting. Sisyphean, even.

But unlike poor Sisyphus, my boulder at least rolled back to a temporary resting place. I went back to work at KHOW, in morning-drive news, which meant arriving at work at 5 A.M., which meant arranging for someone to stay with my kids, and someone to drive them to school. Since I couldn't afford help, several of my women friends offered to stay with us, taking turns in week-to-week shifts, until such time (and they never asked how long) when I could manage on my own.

Remembering all this now, it is not the divorce, debt, and depression that dominate the story. It is that remarkable generosity, translated into overnight stays and carpool shifts, that form the thru-line of the narrative. A narrative punctuated with the odd calls I'd get at those odd hours: "Judy, that's Kerry crying in the background. She refuses to wear socks with her shoes. What would you like me to do?" or "You forgot to sign Kristen's report card. Mind if I fake your signature?" It may not have taken a village, but it sure as hell took a few huts' worth of heart.

So I was back where I'd started, but for a lower salary than I'd made there before, clearly a punishment for leaving in the first place. Now I had not only the clipped coupons and bald tires as motivators, I had humiliation and resentment as well. Hey, whatever works.

I applied to WCBS NewsRadio in New York, not because I was eager to move east, but because I was eager to move up. Unbeknownst to me, they had no room for another reporter, but they sent my resumé and tape over to the folks at the CBS Radio Network. It would never have occurred to me to apply there myself, to presume to make such a grand glissando from minor to major, so when someone with a voice like God's called to say, essentially, "I'm from the Network and I'm here to hire you," I responded, "Yeah, right. Who is this, really?"

A month later, I was back East, getting paid three times as much (no more grocery grief! no more tire terror!), a salary that ensured I could finally support my two daughters, then seven and eight. I'd been awarded primary custody in the divorce but just five hundred dollars a month in child support, so this job was a true godsend. I'd left the kids with my ex-husband for a few weeks so I could house-hunt. I expected that he would put in for a transfer to New York as well, since that is where his company and his family were based. In other words, the trail ahead looked promising but clear.

Cue the cougar.

As with most attacks of this kind, there is rarely any warning, and almost no time to prepare a reaction.

I was alone at a friend's house in New Jersey, where I was staying until I could find a house to buy. As I did every day, I phoned the kids. My youngest daughter, Kerry, answered and immediately burst into tears.

"Daddy says we won't get to live with you until we're eighteen!" she managed to say through her sobs.

"Put him on," I demanded.

I repeated her words back to him and he replied, "You might as well know now, since you'll be served with the papers soon anyway."

Somewhere deep inside, a scream was beginning to form, a shrill scream, and yes, it was the scream of a wild woman. Then he pounced.

"I'm suing you for custody of the kids."

Here is what I remember about that moment.

Everything.

The design of the rug in my friend's kitchen. The gleam of a new toaster oven on the counter. The late afternoon light reflecting on dust dancing in the air. The buzzing of a fly against a window, trying to escape. I especially remember the fly.

I also remember feeling like I was going to die, coupled almost immediately with the awareness of what a cliché that is. That's the little cerebral scribe at work. Observing, assessing, analyzing, even as the adrenal glands are sending out an all-points-bulletin for a full-out, fight-or-flight response. Part of me was aching to flee, even as my gaze was riveted on a similar exercise in futility at the kitchen window. Another part, more frightening than frightened, wanted to do something very, very bad to the person on the other end of the line. This took no translation from any cerebral scribe. It was accompanied by not a whit of metaphor or irony. It was primitive rage, a mother's instinctive response to the threat of her children being taken from her, a rage heightened by the fact that I had left them in his care, trusting his assurances that he supported this move. Rage in its purest form.

Strangely, while I can remember all these emotions and details of my suddenly slo-mo world, I cannot remember what I said in response. That moment and the days that followed, which culminated in a trip back to Denver to face a custody hearing, still stand as my touchstones for "the worst." To this day, if something terrible happens, I think, "But is it as bad as *that?*" So far, only a few moments have come close.

I know other people have touchstones that are far more grievous, such as the death of a child, but whatever the degree of pain involved, these are still important signposts. Without them, there would be no perspective, no yin to the yang, no *story.* However, if someone tries to comfort you in the middle of whatever your personal worst may be with some banality like, "God must have a reason," or, "You're going to be stronger for this," you should feel free to pop them one. If they use the word "closure" in any context, you should feel free to escalate that response, assured in the knowledge that no jury would convict. Besides, an empathic embrace beats banalities every time. Sometimes, as they say, "there are no words." But *if* there are, they should be well crafted and well timed.

This particular chapter ended much better than it began. The judge in Denver ruled that it was absurd to ask me to choose between my children and a job which finally enabled me to support those children. In other words, he ruled in my favor, and I made a mad dash to the airport with my traumatized kids in tow. As the plane took off, Kerry said, "I feel like one of those hostages who got out of Iran."

Well, I thought, at least she's keeping up with current events. I also made a mental note to get us all into family counseling as soon as possible.

My ex-husband soon remarried and moved back East, as we had hoped, putting him in closer contact with the kids. The girls and I moved into a hundred-year-old Victorian home in a small New Jersey town called Metuchen, where I had once worked as a teacher. But now I was working the graveyard shift, 10 P.M. to 5 A.M., driving into New York every night to write and anchor hourly newscasts on CBS radio. This required hiring a series of *au pairs,* including a kleptomaniac who had clearly never heard of Mary Poppins or the fine example she set, and an agoraphobic who was perfect until I made the mistake of paying for her therapy and she learned how great it is to go out. A *lot.*

It had been a trying transition. But I had survived my first cougar attack with my dignity intact. Not to mention all my digits.

But merely surviving such an ambush is not quite the end of it. No, it's a hell of a lot trickier than that. Although it can be terrifically satisfying, in the heat of battle, to cast yourself as the one who has been unjustly set upon (known more commonly as "the victim"), the trek on down the trail becomes downright burdensome if you're still carrying the weight of anger and resentment. In other words, to quote one of those little homilies which so often turn out to be annoyingly true, "Holding a grudge is like taking poison and hoping the other person dies."

So you gotta leave that stuff behind, toss it in the tamaracks, chuck it in the creek (or "crik," as we say in Oregon). Unfortunately, this requires looking at the situation from the *other person's point of view,* which you really, really hate because you're so very fond of *your* point of view. In my case, it meant coming to terms with the fact that my ex-husband was, in fact, afraid of losing his kids. Which made him, at least in this instance, just like me.

Once you arrive at this irritating epiphany, it's not a big leap to the next, which is, essentially, that it's hard to stay angry at someone for doing something you might have done yourself, even if not in exactly the same way. At that point, you are bound to be hit with a deluge of epiphanies, the kind that always seem incredibly deep when they roll through your brain but which always sound incredibly shallow when voiced aloud.

As in: Live and let live. Be here now. Get over it. *Life's too short.*

And as the kids and I got on with our lives, those bumper-sticker epiphanies would have a way of popping up in powerful new ways (that being the nature of epiphanies), reminding me never, ever to take a single moment for granted. Like the time in the middle of the night, a year later, when I was driving to work and caught the tail end of a newscast on the radio. "He was a controversial character in the world of talk radio," said the newscaster, "who had accumulated a number of enemies. To some, his fate came as no surprise."

And I knew. I knew without hearing the identity of the person whose "fate" was being discussed. I rushed into our newsroom to read the wires and there it was: "Controversial radio talk show host Alan Berg was gunned down in his Denver garage after returning from an evening out." Later, we would learn that white supremacists were responsible for the murder. Again, no surprise. Alan used to take regular potshots at the Aryan Nation and others of their ilk. Once, a group of them showed up at the station to threaten him, but he just used the incident as another ingredient to spice up the show. In an interview with *60 Minutes'* Morley Safer shortly before he died, Berg insisted he was aware of the dangers of taunting these people. "Hopefully," he said, "my legal training will prevent me from saying the one thing that will kill me. And I've come awfully close."

Sometimes I wonder if Alan really did understand the power of his own words, the power of the medium. If, as McLuhan said, "the medium *is* the message," then radio has the most personal, and provocative, touch of all.

In the days to come, as I made the transition from radio reporter to commentator, I would have plenty of opportunities to remember that. And I would also remember that, no matter how terrible an emotional ambush might be, it pales next to the real thing.

RADIO NIGHTS

I have been one acquainted with the night.

—Robert Frost

Acquainted, sure. But you aren't really on intimate terms until you've commuted by night.

After an initial year of nearly comatose commuting to an overnight shift that started at 10 P.M. and ended at 6 A.M., I started filling in for Charles Osgood on *The Osgood File,* and was eventually rewarded with my own commentary broadcast, *First Line Report,* during morning "drive time," a time slot people working in radio actually covet.

This coveted shift lasted five years, during which I awoke at 3 A.M. and drove from my home in Metuchen, N.J., to CBS News in Manhattan, where I got down to work writing a radio commentary at 4:30 A.M. For all official purposes, the morning. For all practical and sensory purposes, the middle of the night. REM time. When the only people out and about are either drunk or delivering something—bread, flowers, fish, or news. A handful of people with a single purpose: Get it out before it gets stale.

Trains sleep in the station. Buses doze in the depot. Only the New Jersey Turnpike welcomes the nighttime commuter with open arms. Five years of driving between Exits 10 and 16-E and many hundreds of dollars in tolls qualify me as one who became downright *intimate* with the night.

The New Jersey Turnpike does not get good press. It is not, after all, an especially endearing roadway. Twelve lanes of concrete slashing through one of the bleakest vistas in the United States. From the oil refineries of Linden and Elizabeth to the marshes of Secaucus, the only interesting piece of topography is a large hill, which, as it turns out, is made of garbage. But at night, that hill has a most commanding silhouette.

Even those foulest of New Jersey landmarks, the refineries, are transformed by darkness into twinkling dragons with tongues of fire. But beware that dragon breath. Darkness can't cure everything.

And something else is transformed in the wee-hour commute. Other people who work the night shift tend to be unusually friendly. The reason for these nocturnal niceties, I believe, has something to do with night-shift bonding. Misery really does love company, and I found both at Exit 16-E. Monday through Friday at approximately 4:05 A.M., I rolled up to the toll booths and paid my $1.20. In return, I always got a "Howzitgoin'?" or, on those days when I rolled up at 4:15 or so, a "Running-late-are-we?"

Over time, the "Howzitgoin' " grew into brief conversations about families and vacations and, always, the pains of working weird hours and occasional holidays. *"You* have to work Thanksgiving, *too?"*

I picked up a few loyal listeners, as well, at 16-E. These muses in uniform weren't shy about offering an occasional critique or suggestions of things I might write about. And a bit of warmth to send me on my way.

I needed every bit of camaraderie I could find in those years. While it was an exciting time for my career, it was also a challenging time as a single mother. Juggling the kids' schedule with mine created a sort of schizoid existence, Murphy Brown meets June Cleaver. Shifting from one to the other could be taxing, especially when the shift was unexpected. My kids had an uncanny ability (which they retain to this day) to call me with an "emergency" just before a broadcast. This helped sharpen my diplomatic and deadline skills simultaneously. I'd be typing away (yes, we were still using typewriters), trying to make a 6:25 A.M. deadline for my commentary, when the phone would ring, usually around 6:20.

"Mommy!" (sob, sob, sniffle, sniffle).
"What? What is it? Stop crying; I can't understand you!"
(Still sobbing): "The hamsters got into a fight!"
(Still typing): "Uh huh. The hamsters got into a fight. Okay." (In a voice working hard at changing from irritated to empathic, from Murphy to June): "Caaaalm down, now, honey. It'll be aaaaall right."
"But *Mom!* (sob). One of their eyeballs is (sobsobsniffle) hanging out of the socket!"
(Typing furiously now, my own eyeball on the clock): "Well, shove it back *in* the socket and call me in ten minutes!"

My newsroom colleagues would only hear my side of these conversations, which I imagine were either highly amusing or highly alarming—especially since none of the men in the room ever seemed to receive these kinds of calls. Actually, there was *one* time a male colleague received an emergency call. He'd been recently divorced, as well, and had custody of his kids. I recall that he was about a half-hour away from a deadline for his newscast when the school nurse called to say his son was ill. Without a moment's hesitation, he stood up and said someone else would have to do the newscast because he had to run up to the school to get his sick child.

I remember this as much for the reaction it inspired as for the rarity of such a call. After he'd raced out of the newsroom, everyone started talking about what a *won*derful father he was, how fan*tas*tic that he put his children ahead of his work. Poor *guy,* they said, handling his kids all alone.

Huh? I knew that if I had tried the same thing as this wonderful dad (and he was!) the reaction would have been very, very different. While he was seen as bravely overturning a stereotype, I would be seen as confirming it, this deeply ingrained management suspicion that a single woman raising children alone is not reliable. I was, in fact, an divorced working mother, and we know what Dan Quayle and his army of the morally outraged think of *that.* I'd like to think this attitude has changed over the years, but I'm not real hopeful. Sure, more men may be asking for time off to help take care of their kids, but they often couch it in terms of needing to play "Mr. Mom." Just once, I'd like to hear a woman say, "I've got to play Mr. Dad today and take care of the kids." We can expect that to happen right around the time two women coanchor a major evening newscast.

Meanwhile, working women, especially the single sort, will just have to juggle their guilt right along with their schedules. For my kids, during those early years of my career, there was no such thing as mother-in-the-morning. Often, I was quite astonished to see what they were wearing when I saw them at the end of the day. I'd like to think this whimsical form of self-expression was, in part, what turned them into such creative and independent adults. I may be deluding myself, but then, who *better* to delude me? I once heard someone say that a parent really can't accept credit for the way a kid turns out and refuse to accept blame, as well. Nonsense. I've made it my life's work.

Not that my kids are above pushing those guilt buttons now and then. I suppose their favorite how-we-suffered-for-mom's-career story involves the one Thanksgiving Day when I had to work. No one would switch schedules with me, my family lived far away, so I knew the kids would have to come with me.

Our family really loves this holiday, because it is basically a "promo" for Christmas, without all the stress. Even so, it did not occur to me until years after I'd grown up that the menus for both holidays at our house were *exactly the same:* roast turkey, Mom's special stuffing (which, I was disappointed to learn later, was just the standard mushroom stuffing from *Joy of Cooking*), cranberry sauce out of a can (sometimes with the little rib marks from the can still showing), mashed potatoes, salad, and, for the amen, apple pie.

Nothing special, you might be thinking, but to us, this meal (which I still serve, crumb for crumb, to this day) is a sacrament, a *raison d'être* for the month of November, not to mention an excuse to pig out with friends. So when I announced, with a pathetic attempt at reverse psychology, "Hey, kids, *this* year we get to do something *completely different!*" it was received with about as much enthusiasm as hearing they would be taken to a deserted island and left to starve.

"We have to go to CBS?" said Kristen in disbelief.

"On *Thanksgiving?*" echoed her sister.

"Well, I know it *sounds* bad, but think of it as an adventure. We can go to the Macy's parade first and then you can each play "reporter" with one of the newsroom typewriters and then" (pausing now for dramatic effect), *"then* we can have the special Thanksgiving Day dinner CBS is preparing!"

"In that creepy *cafeteria?*"

"Well, yes . . ."

"All *alone? Just us?"*

They weren't buying the big adventure bit, but we did somehow get through it without terrible trauma, even though to hear them tell it now (which they manage to do, every Thanksgiving), you'd think it scarred their little psyches for life. Oh well, I've got my cougars, they've got theirs. Meanwhile, none of us remembers much about the Macy's parade, which was supposed to be the highlight of the day, except that it was freezing cold and that when Donnie Osmond appeared on top of a turkey float, someone behind us muttered, "Now, *that's* redundant." On the other hand, it's a perfect example of how even the worst experience can offer up a memorable quote.

Even after my radio schedule changed, some years later, to a basic 9-to-5 day, I was still struggling to pull off the dicey handoff from no-nonsense to nurturing. The enormous effort this required recently came back to me when the dean of a university that was considering me for a job called my old CBS radio news director for a recommendation. When he'd heard enough kudos, the dean said, "Tell me the worst thing you can remember about her."

"Well," said my former boss, "she used to do the 5:00 newscast in her coat."

To him, that was a sign that I couldn't wait to leave work and was, from his point of view, reflective of a poor end-of-the-day attitude. What he never knew was that if I didn't bolt for the door at precisely 5:05 P.M., I wouldn't make my 5:25 train to New Jersey, and if I didn't make that train, I couldn't make dinner for my kids, and if I couldn't make dinner for my kids, then my whole belief system would collapse. Which basically came down to: We *will* eat together every single night, just as my family did, even though my mother stayed home all day whipping up dishes that always seemed to involve cream of mushroom soup, because if we don't do this, my children will take drugs, commit felonies, and prompt everyone I know to say, *"See?* THIS is what happens when a woman tries to have it all!"

And, of course, you can't. Have it all, that is. But getting to write a commentary every morning that reached some three million listeners came awfully close. It combined everything I loved about storytelling: weaving personal and public themes together to connect with others in a way that would not otherwise be possible.

Sometimes the connections were a little more intimate than I had hoped for. I'd often meet listeners who would feel compelled to tell me exactly what they were doing every morning while tuned in to *First Line Report.* "I take a shower with you every day," leered one man I met at a party. "My wife and I were having great sex one morning," said another, his wife beaming at his side, "and we had to stop because we both started laughing so hard at what you were saying."

"Do you remember what the piece was about?" I asked, as visions of radio interruptus danced in my head.

"Oh, sure," replied the husband. "It was that bit you did about

Oliver North's nickname in the Iran Contra operation. What was it?"

"Steelhammer," giggled his wife. I thanked them and excused myself, even though I don't think they noticed, what with visions of steelhammers dancing in *their* heads. But I couldn't help but wonder: How many other folks were copulating to commentary? Not that I really wanted to know. This was clearly TMI, as my kids would say: Too much information.

First Line Report was supposed to be tied to a breaking story, or at least as topical a subject as we could find. When I rolled into the newsroom at 4:30 A.M., my radio producer would already have gleaned a number of items for my perusal. Between 4:30 and 6:25, when *First Line Report* aired, I'd choose a topic, come up with my own insights and analysis, and then craft it all into a coherent essay, sometimes mixed with portions of taped interviews conducted under the same horrific deadline pressure. All this required a near-lethal dose of caffeine and a somewhat questionable talent for taking complicated subjects and reducing them to a simple essence lasting no more than two-and-a-half minutes. Even so, it's possible to squeeze in at least one decent insight in that amount of time, and I almost never tired of the challenge. The best part was that I had the final word on what went on the air, a luxury I would never know again. A desk editor would check the commentary for facts, and my producer would now and then gingerly suggest I might want to phrase something a little more delicately: "Do you *really* want to say 'President Reagan is either dumb or lying?' " she'd inquire, invariably saving me from myself.

While I was given a lot of latitude on subject matter, more

often than not *First Line Report* involved a "hard news" issue, sometimes requiring early morning interviews that rousted famous folk from their slumber. These were the days before answering machines were ubiquitous and people actually picked up the receiver when it rang at, say, 5:30 in the morning. I'd like to say I bravely shouldered this unpleasant task all by myself, but I would no doubt be pummeled by the various producers who did so much of the dialing and cajoling. Even so, I became the only reporter I know who started interviews with an apology: "Hello, this is Judy Muller, with CBS News in New York. I know how early this is. I'm so sorry. Did we wake you?"

Disingenuous, sure, but terrific training for future interviews requiring anything from a smidgen of supplication to grotesque groveling. Now that I think of it, terrific training for a future booker on a TV magazine show (a job category that didn't really exist then, back when making such intrusive calls was still considered something that *required* an apology).

The advantage of these predawn raids was that the interview subjects were less guarded. They did not have time, as one review of our broadcast put it, "to shower and shave their responses." Perhaps that's why the late Senator Henry "Scoop" Jackson gave new meaning to his nickname when we woke him up one morning. He disclosed that Henry Kissinger would be named to head a presidential commission on Central America, something that doesn't seem terribly important or even memorable now, but was, trust me, something of a scoop that day. We also had the opportunity to be the first to inform a Nobel Prize winner of his just-announced honor, and to inform the father of an American pilot captured in Syria that his son had just been released.

Other notables who seemed more than willing to talk at these awkward hours included Jesse Jackson, who took a mere minute to warm up before launching into his preacher patois; Claus Von Bulow, still dripping from his shower (he shared this with us a bit too eagerly, I thought), enthusiastically speculating on who might be cast to play him in an upcoming film; and Desmond Tutu, who answered his own phone, which so surprised my producer that she spit a bagel clear across the room.

There were disadvantages as well to this pre-reveille deadline pressure. Some of our subjects weren't terribly lively, something that became more true as we headed west, across the time zones. I once interviewed an astronomer in California about a special telescope that was in the news that morning. Unfortunately, it was 2:30 A.M. when we woke him up. Somewhere in the middle of the interview he stopped responding to my questions. He was, in fact, snoring. After that episode, we urged our interview-ees to place themselves in the upright position prior to takeoff.

We often took risks with this broadcast, which probably sprang from our relative inexperience with, and our utter disregard for, the politics of network news. One morning, we decided to take on the controversial topic of how a news organization covers itself. The day before, CBS News had released the "Benjamin Report," an in-house investigation of a documentary about Vietnam that had prompted a $120-million libel suit by General William Westmoreland. The in-house probe had been conducted by Burton Benjamin, an old-school producer with a reputation for old-fashioned integrity. It was unusually blunt in detailing the way the documentary's producers had, in fact, violated a number of CBS news standards, including juxtaposing answers with questions that did not specifically elicit those answers. CBS had prepared this report for internal use only, but was forced to release it under court order, and almost every media outlet was reporting it. Everyone, that is, except CBS News. We couldn't even find a copy of the report in our newsroom. So we gulped hard, and waited until 5:30 A.M. to call the president of CBS News, Van Gordon Sauter. We asked him about the role CBS News should play in reporting on itself.

To our surprise, he was not grumpy about being asked. To our even greater surprise, he said he thought CBS *should* be reporting the story.

M U L L E R :   *Why, then, do you think that neither the* Evening News with Dan Rather, Nightwatch, *or any of the radio hourlies have touched the story?*

S A U T E R :   *That's a decision that would have to be answered by those individual elements.*

M U L L E R :   *Do you believe the release of the Benjamin Report will jeopardize future internal investigations for all news organizations? Will people be afraid to speak frankly for fear their comments will end up in court, in print, and on the air?*

S A U T E R :   *Once you lose that capability of that confidentiality, those journalistic examinations will end up being done by lawyers under the cloak of privilege and not by journalists, and I think in that process there is something very vital that's being lost.*

His remarks were prescient. Lawyers have since become indispensable players in news divisions, and outspoken internal debate is rarely encouraged. And yes, something vital has been lost.

While Sauter reacted with good cheer to our early morning

interview, not so Dan Rather. On a particularly slow news day, the best issue we could find that was suitable for a commentary was a story about a lawsuit Rather and CBS had just won. It involved a so-called "ambush interview" he had conducted with a reluctant subject for a *60 Minutes* story. Since he had won this case, we thought we might be able to persuade him to talk about the kinds of interview techniques required for investigative journalism. We thought, in our naivete, that he might even *enjoy* talking about it.

My producer waited until the last possible moment to make the call to Rather's home. I believe it was close to 6 A.M. when she woke him up. He told her, in a sleepy but polite Texas drawl, that he didn't want to comment because he had turned down a number of requests for interviews the night before and didn't want to give the impression that he was playing favorites with his own organization. Sorry, he said. My producer apologized (the cliché "apologized profusely" was meant for moments like this), said she hoped he could get back to sleep, hung up and screamed, *"Start writing!"*

I don't remember what our fallback topic was. I only remember that I had about twenty minutes to write an essay about it. And I also remember the phone call in the middle of that madness, a call from the president of the radio news division.

"Did somebody there wake up the anchorman?" he thundered.

"Um, yes," I replied, "we did. How did you know?"

"Because," he said, "he just woke *me* up to complain about it. He's coming in to see me this morning. And he wants *your heads!"*

Literally, I wondered, as in John the Baptist? Or metaphorically, as in our jobs? And if he was upset, why hadn't he said so?

Somehow we got on the air with something. About 9 A.M., Rather stormed by my desk in the newsroom and went straight into this executive's office. For the next half hour, we could hear raised voices behind the closed door. Meanwhile, out in the newsroom, newspeople did what they do so well in newsrooms everywhere: pretend they aren't listening even as they strain to take in every detail. My producer and I were stunned. Of all the people we had ever awakened, from Nobel Prize winners to convicted felons, no one had ever expressed such outrage.

And then the door opened. Rather stormed right back out. He clearly had not been mollified. I was called in.

"He wanted you and your producer punished," said our boss, "but I told him that you were just doing your job with a difficult deadline. I told him he would have done the same thing in your position."

"You *did?*" (To this day, I still wonder if that's exactly how he put it. He had reverentially referred to Rather as "the anchorman," after all).

And so we were not punished. At least not overtly. But in echoes of that suburban shunning I'd known long ago, Rather didn't speak to me for about a year, a silence broken only after I wrote a piece about flyfishing for *Sports Illustrated*. "Judy," he penned on his personal stationery, "I've . . . read the *SI* piece. It is first-rate. Congratulations! —Dan." From then on, we would trade salutations when we'd pass each other in the long, narrow corridor between radio and TV-land, and sometimes we'd even pause to speak. But only about fishing. It was an odd relationship, one that would figure in my decision, down the line, to go to ABC.

Meanwhile, radio still presented some interesting challenges. The year I was assigned to spend some time on the Bush presidential campaign, 1988, was the year CBS Radio decided it could no longer afford to send technical engineers to accompany reporters on the campaign trail. I realize that, to modern radio reporters, the old ways must sound both exotic and wimpy, much like being accompanied by Sherpas for a day hike. But back then, at least to Luddites like myself, the change represented technological terror in the extreme. It meant lugging around enough equipment to herniate an elephant, what with microphones and mixers and tapes and recorders and batteries and wires and clips and all the other technical flapdoodle that seemed to be required.

On the press plane, I was seated next to a radio guy from another network who had all sorts of mysterious gadgets inside a large bag. He would stick his head down into this bag, wiggle a few things around, speak into it as though it were his own personal sound booth, and abracadabra, coherent reportage would magically emerge, which he would then feed over a bulky cellular phone he carried everywhere. I, in turn, had no cell phone (they were still a relatively new luxury), had no bag of tricks, had nothing but a pair of "alligator clips" to feed stories over a phone. Which meant *finding* a phone, one with a mouthpiece that could be disassembled, usually under gut-wrenching deadline pressure, all the while listening to the press bus revving its engines and knowing the campaign waits for no one.

I'd also been equipped with a boom mike, the better to reach the candidate when the press went into gang bang mode, which was most of the time. Problem was, the boom mike was broken and would continually droop, requiring constant adjustments so the candidate would not sound as though he were petering out, like the mike itself. At the same time, I'd be trying to manipulate a tape recorder and take notes.

This might have marked one of the first times that a career in television began to look attractive to me. The television reporters, I noticed, were accompanied by a producer, a cameraman, and an audio technician. TV, I thought, is a many-sherpa'd thing. I specifically remember one woman correspondent who actually wore *heels* every day. It's not so much that I *wanted* to wear heels; I simply wanted to know I *could*.

By the end of a day, with perhaps as many as five campaign stops in as many as three states, I'd lose track of time zones and even cities. I seriously offended a local reporter who had turned out with great enthusiasm to hear Bush deliver a speech, a speech the national press corps had heard so often that some reporters were able to develop some pretty amazing lip-synching skills. We had just exited the press plane to wait on the tarmac where Bush was to appear for his remarks. Loaded down with my usual ton of equipment, including the erectile-dysfunctioning boom mike, I turned my weary besneakered feet in this young reporter's direction and asked, "Excuse me, is this Springfield, Missouri, or Springfield, Illinois?"

He was appalled. It was as though we were waiting for the pope and I had asked if this was Rome, Georgia, or Rome, Italy.

"Missouri," came the huffy response, accompanied by a glare that spoke volumes about the sacredness of this event in his mind. In his hand, he gripped a page of typewritten questions, no doubt carefully constructed in great anticipation of this chance to ask *the question* that would elicit *the answer* that would make news. For a moment, I actually felt ashamed at my weary cynicism. Even today, when that cynicism threatens to crop up, as it will after observing politicians for any length of time, I like to think of that eager reporter, hoping to get a word in edgewise, hoping to make a difference. At that moment in Springfield, Missouri, I actually started rooting for the guy, hoping he might get his chance.

Not a chance. Once in full stampede, herd journalism gives no quarter to the weak. I last saw him at the edge of the pack, jumping up and down, his neatly typed questions clutched tightly in hand, screaming *"Mr. Vice President?"* I wonder if he ever sharpened his elbows and hardened his resolve. If so, he's probably enjoying a good career. If not, he's probably a really nice guy.

If there was a pecking order on the tarmac, it paled in comparison to that aboard the plane. Print and network television reporters sat up front, radio reporters toward the rear with the camera crews, who liked it that way, because that's where the bar was. And if I'd had any doubt about the ghettoization of radio, it was obliterated when one of the campaign aides strode to the back of the plane at the end of one particularly trying day and said to me, "I hate to tell you this, but CBS News is delinquent in its payments for its space on this plane. We're going to have to bump you when we land in Montana."

It was night. It was snowing like a sonofabitch. And for an unpaid bill, I'd be bumped in Billings? While I could appreciate the alliteration, I could not fathom why, of the many CBS personnel aboard, I had been singled out. And then it hit me: I'm radio, the bottom of the food chain.

I was mustering up the courage to be the Rosa Parks of Radio (I know, I was already in the back of this bus, but at least I wasn't going to let them throw me off it, which should count

for something), when CBS Correspondent Bob Schieffer inter-
vened.

"*Hold on,* there," he said to the aide. And he made a call to
someone in New York: "Hey, they're trying to throw Judy Muller
off the plane in Montana because the network hasn't paid its bill
yet." (Muffled sounds on the other end.) "Judy Muller. You know,
from radio." (Mmfff, mmmfff.) "Right, okay. So you'll assure
these folks that the check is in the mail? All right then."

I don't know who he called. But I do know that it was because a TV guy stood up for me that I did not get the boot in a
blizzard. Yes, TV was looking very attractive, indeed.

And even more so by the time I covered the Bush inaugura-
tion in January 1989. The scene: the Kennedy Center in Wash-
ington. The event: one of many inaugural balls. The problem: five
thousand people from five states crammed in so tightly it formed
human gridlock—literally. For hours, they stood cheek to cheek,
both kinds, waiting for the First Couple to arrive. No one could
get near the bar, no one could get near the restrooms, No one
could move, period. Much less dance. It was getting ugly. When
I arrived, in formal evening dress (a requirement for reporters
covering inaugural balls), my sharp reporter's instinct told me I
had a problem here. I was to be on the air, live, in just twenty
minutes, but the radio engineer who would make this possible
was at least fifty feet away, on the other side of a very long camera platform, a platform surrounded by irritated people with
nowhere to go, but an increasing urge to go, if you get my drift.

So I hiked up my floor-length gown and took the path of
least resistance. I got down on my hands and knees, and crawled
under the camera platform to reach my engineer on the other
side, leaving a trail of sequins in my wake. All the while, cam-

eramen above me were yelling, "Hey, you idiot, watch those cables!" and some other things that are really too ugly to reprise. Bush finally arrived and spoke for three minutes, tops, and we got it on the air. Afterward, I looked up and saw all the television reporters standing on the platform looking glamourous and unruffled, the groomed above the groundlings, all their sequins intact.

So it's safe to say that the seeds of discontent had been solidly planted by the time Charlie Osgood decided he wanted to do four *Osgood Files* each morning, rather than just one, and the CBS radio hierarchy moved my commentary to the middle of the day. This improved my sleeping patterns, but was hell on my ratings. I also became one acquainted with the day, and a commute that left a lot to be desired. Once I was on the day shift, I missed all that nighttime camaraderie. As just one more bit of mass in mass transit, I was no longer captain of my fate. Ensign, maybe. That is, I was in control of some things: which train to catch, which car to sit in.

Friends assured me there would be compensations. Think of the interesting people you'll meet, they said. So I made the effort. The very first day, I gave my warmest "good morning" to a woman standing on the platform at Metuchen. She proceeded to tell me every detail of her recent hysterectomy. She followed me onto the train, sat down next to me. By the time we reached Penn Station in Manhattan, she was just coming out of recovery. I began to understand why all those people were reading newspapers.

In my brief experience as a daytime commuter, I remember only one time when the people around me dropped those papers, turned to a neighbor, and actually spoke. Enroute to New

York, in the marshes of Secaucus, in the shadow of the mountain of garbage, the train broke down. And so did all the barriers. People began comparing notes about all the times they'd been stuck on a train, began their own daytime version of Misery Loves Company.

But moments later, the train started, conversation stopped, and faces were once again hidden by newsprint. It occurred to me that I had more human contact at exit 16-E in the middle of the night than I had on a train packed with hundreds of people in broad daylight.

I remember the last time I drove through that toll booth. A surprised voice said, "I heard you were moving to the day shift."

"I am," I replied. "This is my last night."

"In that case," he said, "this one's on me." And he handed back my money.

LOVE
IN THE
AFTERNOON

*(Between 2 and 2:30 If My Schedule Allows and
Jibes with His and the Kids Aren't Home from School
and I'm Lucky Enough to Find a Lover Who Thinks
Sunshine on Cellulite Is an Interesting Look)*

W hen I got divorced, at the age of thirty-four, I had this notion that I would simply pick up, or get picked up, where I had left off. This was, of course, delusional. But understandable, considering my last reference point, a hormonally happy time when attractive, bright young men roamed the land and picker-uppers could be choosers, a time known as *college*. The postdivorce reality was something else entirely; where once there had been a plethora of eligible, interesting guys, there was now a pathetic collection of troubled, neurotic, commitment-phobes trying to appear just the opposite in personal ads, such as:

"Ruggedly handsome"
(ruts to rival the Grand Canyon),
"Looking to share intimate nights at home"
(really, really cheap),
"Love to take romantic walks on the beach"
(will say whatever it takes to get laid),
"Smoking ok, drinking ok, bestiality ok, but no children!"
(needs no translation).

This is not to say that I haven't managed to meet some terrific guys over the years who, for one reason or another, just didn't work out for the long haul. Some of them (well, okay, two of them) are still good friends. But in between these Significant Others, there have been some close encounters with a few Insignificant Others, including a fellow I met (YES, I ADMIT IT, SO CALL ME DESPERATE!) through his personal ad.

A quick aside, if I may: In keeping with our overarching theme of how the art of storytelling can impose some sanity on life's chaos, it's important, I think, to point out that, *here again*(!), we have an example of how the most humiliating situation can be transformed into, well, a humiliating *story*. I like to believe there is a difference. I *have* to believe there is a difference.

This particular humiliating story, sort of an O. Henry-meets-J. Seinfeld kind of tale, begins in the early eighties when the kids and I were sitting in the backyard in New Jersey having a good chuckle over the personal ads in *New York* magazine. Keep in mind that this was light years before single people started meeting on the Internet, making the whole thing socially acceptable, as in the movie *You've Got Mail!*. This was, socially speaking, the *Dark Time,* when the movie of reference was *Looking for Mr. Goodbar,* when it was unseemly to actually admit you might take such ads seriously (*"Oh no,"* you'd laugh gaily when someone would catch you perusing the personals, "I just read them for laughs. Haha!"), when the odds of meeting a great guy, between working a full-time job that begins at 4 A.M. and racing to the orthodontist and Brownie meetings and soccer practice, were about as good as the odds of getting hit by lightning not twice but thrice. But I digress.

So there we were, perusing the ads for laughs, *really,* when one caught my eye. "Wait a minute," I said to the kids, "this one doesn't sound so bad." It was an ad placed by a professor at NYU (if memory serves), and it was witty and smart. I actually considered it for a moment, thought, *"Naaaah,* I'm not that desperate *yet,"* and forgot about it. But unbeknownst to me, my daughters, then nine and ten years old, sent off one of my publicity photos from CBS with my phone number on the back of it. When they told me about it later, as in several weeks later, I had to laugh. After all, the guy had never called. I had been rejected on the basis of an eight-by-ten glossy, which is, let's face it, about the best you're *ever* going to look.

Now fast-forward several years. A serious relationship had just ended (note the use of the nonaccusational passive voice, a real sign of my personal growth, if I do say so myself) and the concept of a superficial relationship was something I was willing to entertain. And so, I found myself once again perusing the personals in *New York* magazine. Again, I spotted an interesting ad which read, to the best of my recollection, something along the lines of: "Tall, attractive, liberal SWM, works in Democratic politics, in search of funny, intelligent SWF. Children no problem. Republicans need not apply."

This guy has possibilities, I thought to myself. And so, in a furtive moment, I mailed off a note, no picture, and a phone number. He called. We lunched. I yawned. Oh sure, the guy was all the things he'd advertised. He had simply *failed* to advertise the humorless part. "Oh well," I thought, as we got up to leave, "nothing ventured." That's when I saw him pull out a small notebook and begin scribbling in it. He caught my quizzical expression. "Sorry," he said, "but if I don't write down my impressions right away, I get all the women who answered my ad confused in my mind."

I know what you're thinking right about now. You're thinking, "Ah, so *this* is the humiliating part."

No, actually, it's not. This is the outrageous part.

"You've *got* to be kidding," I said, indignantly. "Do you have some sort of rating system?"

"Oh, just a simple letter grade. Maybe a remark or two to jog my memory."

Clearly, these are the moments that call for a brilliant retort, a withering rejoinder, like the one Marcia Clark had for F. Lee Bailey in the Simpson trial when she held up a glove and said "Size *small,* must be Mr. Bailey's." Granted, it was her *only* good moment, but memorable, nonetheless.

Unfortunately, my best retorts spring into my head hours, even days, later. A friend of mine calls this the "driving-home-in-the-car-comeback." And so, instead of a droll insult worthy of Dorothy Parker, I said, "Oh, *yeah?* And what grade did *I* get?" I like to think this was at least delivered in a tone in which the additional phrase "you jerk" was implied.

"An A-minus."

"Minus? *Minus?*"

"Well, you *do* live in New Jersey."

Needless to say, this was not a love connection. This was a disconnection. Even as he was writing his "remarks," I was writing him off. I didn't feel a need to verbally express this rejection. Well, maybe I did feel a need but I couldn't think of a really pithy parting insult. So I went home and promptly forgot about him.

Until the phone rang a week later. It was him, although at

first, I didn't recognize the name. "Oh," I said, when I realized who it was. "Oh, sure. Hi."

"I felt it only fair to let you know," he said, with a touch of condescension.

"Fair to let me know what?" I responded, with a touch of apprehension.

"Well, I've given this some thought, and I just don't think this would work out."

"*What* wouldn't work out?"

"Us."

(Us? *Us?*)

"As I said, you live in New Jersey and I just don't think we'd be compatible."

"I never thought we *would* be," I sputtered, sounding defensive now, thinking, "Is there anything worse than being dumped by someone you've already dumped, only you failed to tell him as much, so now he gets to make you look like the dumpee?"

Well, yes, in fact, there is.

Just as I was searching for the right remark to deflate this date-from-hell once and for all, he added, almost as an aside, "By the way, I thought you said at lunch the other day that you had never answered one of these ads before."

"That's right."

"Well, then, why does my best friend have your CBS publicity photo from a few years ago?"

This would be the humiliating part.

What were the odds? I thought. I mean, of all the people in New York, these two guys are friends? What followed was an embarrassing attempt, unbelievable even to my own ears, to explain how that picture was sent as a prank, an innocent prank, not intended as a serious response to a personal ad, no-no-never, all the while knowing he wasn't buying a single word. In fact, I bet he believes to this day that I peppered Manhattan with eight-by-ten glossies, possibly air-dropped from a news chopper. Perhaps he'll read this and know, at last, that I was telling the truth.

Not that I care, of course.

Given the reality of my situation as a single mom living in the provinces and working extraordinarily weird hours which rendered me fairly comatose by Friday evening, I suppose it's a wonder I had any social life at all. But I did. All it took was strategic planning on par with a full-scale NATO offensive. For all those single moms out there who are conscious, as I was, of not wanting to march a parade of men through their kids' lives but, at the same time, needing to have some sort of adult "relationship," a euphemism if I ever heard one, please know that it is possible. The means to this end can be summed up in one word: the *sleepover.*

And by sleepover, I mean your kids sleeping over at some other kid's house. This takes some tricky maneuvering, especially when you have two daughters, as I did, each with her own set of friends.

Unfortunately, kids cannot be trusted to make these arrangements in order to jibe with your special needs. First, they have no idea you have "special needs," nor do they want to know. Even kids who live with both parents do not want to know. Did *you* want to know what *your* parents were doing? Of course not. The very thought of it makes you vomit, even today. Married couples have it much easier, of course, since the kids *expect* them to disappear now and then into their own bedroom. And any strange outbursts invoking the name of God can always be chalked up to prayer.

A single parent faces a tougher challenge; you can wait until the little buggers go to sleep (which will take an interminable amount of time since they will immediately sense you *want* them to) and then try with all your might to remain utterly silent, lest you should wake them and then face the even bigger challenge of explaining that, no, there was *not* a cougar in Mommy's bedroom (see Chapter 1). Or, you can ship them out to someone else's house. Clearly, there's no contest between these two options. In fact, I believe the concept of the sleepover was probably invented by some crazed single mom dying to get in touch with her inner cougar.

And so, every now and then, I would call other mothers with a not-so-subtle proposal.

"I was thinking it would be nice if the girls could get together Saturday night. What do you think? Yes? Terrific. Whoops! Wait a minute, I just remembered. I have a friend coming into town. Really? You wouldn't mind? Well, okay, but I'll tell you what, if you take them this Saturday, I'll reciprocate the following weekend. No need? But I insist. Well, okay, if you're sure. Terrific. I'll have her there by 6:00."

The more children you have, of course, the more complicated this becomes. And obviously the approach has to vary now and then. I mean, how many "friends" from out of town can one person have? And now and then, of course, you do have to reciprocate and host an overnight gaggle of gigglers in *your* basement. But it's a small price to pay for an occasional, and I do mean occasional, evening to call your own.

As for the afternoon tryst referred to at the beginning of this chapter, that was just a shameless way to get your attention. Your tipoff should have been the self-deprecating reference to cellulite. I live in California, where cellulite is not allowed. This should have led you to a simple syllogism: Californians have no cellulite. The author lives in California. Ergo, the author has a perfect body. Pass it on.

At any rate, afternoon affairs are very difficult to pull off. The only one I ever heard of that was truly successful involved a UPS man in Montana, who apparently was delivering a tad more than the job description called for. The woman accepting those afternoon deliveries was married to the owner of a diner in a very small town, a place so desolate, in fact, that you had to figure that everyone who lived there must have descended from pioneers who, when their wagons broke down, didn't know how to fix them. A few hundred more miles to the west and they would've been in paradise.

I happened to spend a little bit of time in this town covering a story, and so had the opportunity, if you can call it that, to "dine" at this establishment quite often. I remember it most for its absolute failure to offer any dish that might qualify as a vegetable, other than that Reagan favorite, ketchup. One of my colleagues once asked the owner if there was any chance of getting something in a shade of green with his dinner. The irritated response: "Well, I've got a big can of peas back there, but I hate to open it for just one person."

At any rate, this woman and her husband had both attached their names to this diner, so when I asked some local folk one night about the whereabouts of the female half of this partnership, they looked somewhat embarrassed and said, "She's not here anymore. She went and ran off with the UPS man." This was pronounced "ups," as in ups and downs.

Her spontaneous departure was clearly seen as something much too scandalous for polite conversation. But it sounded pretty romantic to me, a sort of modern take on *Shane,* only in this version, the wife has the good sense to accompany her hero as he takes that long and winding road out of town.

Unfortunately, Shane does not ride into the suburbs of New Jersey.

And so, you have to keep on "dating," an unnatural act for anyone over the age of eighteen, until the Real Thing comes along. Life does get a little bit easier, schedule-wise, once you enter into that state which goes by the decidedly unromantic moniker of "Committed Relationship." I prefer to go with the old-fashioned appellation "Love," although I'd be hard-pressed to define just what it is. And certainly, when you're on the downside of a failed love affair, it's easy to slide into cynicism, to believe, as writer Dan Greenburg once put it, that "love is the self-delusion we manufacture to justify the trouble we take to have sex." But having loved, and lost, a few times, I'd like to think it's much more than that. I realize that the very phrase "like to think" smacks of self-delusion, but we're talking about hope here, and everyone needs a dollop now and then. Otherwise, why keep trying? There are required time-outs between rounds, of course, those recuperations from romance when the protective walls go back up in short order, when you begin to understand what Billie Holiday meant when she said, "Don't threaten me with love, baby." But no matter how many times you hear people say, "That's it, no more, I can't go through it ever again," they still manage to do exactly that. Perhaps it *can* all be reduced to sex, but that wouldn't make for a very good story. Do you think anyone would cry at the end of *Casablanca* if Rick turned to Ilsa on the airport tarmac and said, "To hell with Laszlo. Let's get it on one more time?"

And anyway, it's pretty near impossible for a single mom to be self-delusional in the romance department, at least as long as the kids are around. Perhaps because they know that every suitor is a potential stepdad, representing one more layer of authority than they really feel is necessary, they are much pickier than you yourself might be, sex-starved creature that you are. My daughters, for example, had an incredible instinct for homing in on the one thing that might be unconsciously bothering me about a guy. When Kristen was about eleven years old, I introduced her to someone I'd dated a few times, a man I'd met in a running club. Kristen had decided to come along for a jog that day. As he came loping toward us, I said, "There he is now."

"That guy coming this way?"

"Yep."

"The one with the little head?"

"What do you mean?"

"Oh, come *on,* Mom, that man's head is way too small for his body."

I'm not saying that this one little remark made the crucial difference. There were some other setbacks, including the night he leaned across the table in a restaurant, took my hands in his, and whispered, "Have we talked yet about Jesus?" But I would have to admit, superficial hussy that I am, that from the moment she pointed it out to me, he became the man with the incredible shrinking head. A few more weeks and it was over.

Once the girls themselves got old enough to start dating, I was able to exact my revenge for these outbursts of honesty. In our family, "damning with faint praise" is something of an art form, and it is often much more effective than a straight-out critique. "He seems pretty nice" is much more deadly, and effective, than "What in the world do you see in that jerk?" My big brother used the faint-praise technique on me when I was a teenager, and let me tell you, it was a killer. Now that I think of it, he uses it on me as an adult, and it still works. So if your daughter suddenly decides to flex those adolescent muscles of rebellion and brings home a guy who looks like he's one misdemeanor away from serious jail time, a simple "He seems nice, dear" will destroy whatever romantic fantasy she might be harboring about her rebel without a cause. *Nice?* No self-respecting adolescent wants anything to do with *nice.*

To be fair, the girls went out with some great guys, "nice" in the most sincere sense of the word. But single parents, I think, tend to be overly protective about these things. And the dating years seem to come along so suddenly, especially when you're still grappling with the abrupt and untimely return of your own.

It seemed as though, one day I was answering a timid knock at the door, looking down and seeing little Billy holding a flower and saying, in a shy voice, "Is Kristen home?" (How cute, I thought, he has a crush on my daughter! And he's just half her size!)

And the next day (well, maybe it was a couple of years), Big Bad Bill (AKA Little Billy) would be pounding on the door, demanding to see Kristen in a voice at least three octaves lower with a hormonally crazed leer that seemed to be locked on all targets at breast level. (He wants my daughter! And he's twice her size!)

These were the moments when my mother would start channeling through me, unbidden. I remember once when Kerry was parked out in front of the house one evening with her boyfriend, and we were waiting for her to come inside so we could eat dinner. Her older sister, ever on the lookout to score an advantage, said, "You know, Mom, I don't think she's coming in any time soon. The windows on the car are fogging up."

I, in turn, trying to be the open-minded modern mom, said, "Oh, give her a few moments. I'm sure she'll be right in. She knows what time it is. And meanwhile, stop staring out the window."

A few more moments passed. And then some more.

"Mom," said Kristen, "they're still going at it. Maybe you should do something."

"Kristen," I responded patiently, "when I was a girl, my mother used to flick the porch light on and off when I was outside with a boyfriend. I promised myself right then and there that, when I had children, I would *never* humiliate them that way. And you know what, Kristen?"

"What?"

"You are now going to see me break that promise."

And with that, I made a beeline to the front door, flicked the porch light on and off in a frenzy. Kerry was angry, her sister was smug, and I was humbled. I had learned that, when it comes to raising teenagers, you can never say never, especially when it comes to trying to resist morphing into your mom at critical moments.

As for my own romantic interludes, I have, at least, learned some valuable lessons my mother could never have passed on, or even dreamed of, mostly because she remained happily married for fifty years to one terrific guy and never had to deal with the horrors of adult dating. Or well-meaning friends who want to "fix you up," which sounds way too much like car repair for my taste. "Not to worry, we'll have 'er fixed up in no time!"

I realize that by stating this publicly, the odds are good that I'll never be fixed up again, a risk I think I'm willing to take. I've never been personally fond of anything with the word "blind" attached to it, unless it's venetian. I can't remember one blind date that actually worked out. Worse, it forces you to see the friends who arranged the meeting in a new, and not always flattering, light. "What were they thinking of?" is your first thought. "I'm going to kill them" is your second.

Consider just one example. After securing my permission, my friend Joanne gave my phone number to a male friend of hers who happened to be a comedy writer. I'm sure she was thinking, "Hey, two funny people . . . what could go wrong?" We met in Manhattan for drinks before going to Lincoln Center for the opera. Promising enough. As we walked into the elevator to ride up to our seats, I was thinking, "Joanne really came through!"

That's when he said it.

In an elevator jammed with the tuxed and gowned members of the audience (ours, at that moment), he said, loud enough for all to hear, "One thing you should know. I've had a vasectomy."

And I did what any coward would do at such a moment. I pretended I didn't know him. I started to do what those around me did: look around curiously, as if to say, "What's this guy talking about?" Even so, I can't remember any elevator ride ever taking that long, before or since. When we finally emerged on the upper tier of Lincoln Center, and got out of earshot of the others, I turned to him and said, *"Why on earth would you say something like that?"*

"I always like to tell women early in a relationship," he replied, "because they may want children."

It was early in the relationship, all right. I'd known him about an hour and a half.

And so the world's longest elevator ride was followed by the world's longest opera, sitting next to a man with the world's longest arm. No matter how I shifted in my seat, he kept trying to rub the back of my neck. But as oblivious as he was, he was not so self-absorbed that he missed the chill that even the most passionate aria could not dispel. And so he never called again. But I knew that, if he did, I could always say, "I'm sorry, I don't think it would work out. I want to have children."

Blind dates are not the only dangerous intersections single women might want to avoid. Even more treacherous are the guys who "are going through a divorce." This is an area where self-delusion can easily get a hold of your vulnerable little heart and twist it around to the point where you find yourself saying to your friends, "I'm seeing a man who's going through a divorce."

You are not. You are seeing a married man.

That's the truth, no matter how long he's been separated. If you are involved in such a relationship, however, you do not want to hear that. If you've been in the desert for awhile, you don't want to be told that the water is really a mirage. Even so, I offer a handy translation guide for those who are open to hearing it, even though I certainly wasn't at the time.

Him: "It's all over but the legalities. I'm working on getting a divorce."

Translation: He's married.

Him: "We've been looking for a mediator, so we can work out the divorce without lawyers."

Translation: He hates confrontation. And, he's married.

Him: "Well, we've hired a mediator. But he's also a part-time roofing contractor, and since it's the rainy season, it may be awhile before he gets to us."

Translation: He's very married. And if you buy this, as I did, you need intense and immediate therapy.

Him (after several months or even years): "I don't understand why the technicality of a divorce is so important to you. I don't live with her. I rarely see her. These things are complicated, economically speaking. Maybe you and I just have a different definition of 'marriage.' "

Translation: It depends on what the meaning of "is" is. And, oh yes, he's married.

You can save yourself a lot of trouble, of course, not to mention a lot of translating, if you avoid these no-win situations in the first place. If you listen to this stuff long enough, respect goes out the window, and love is bound to follow. If you stand up to it, and say, "Call me when you're really free," know that he may very well take the path of least resistance; that is, he will simply replace you with someone who hasn't yet learned the language of "going through a divorce." This will break your heart, but should strengthen your resolve.

There is one other possibility, but you must be very careful never to think of it as a probability. You can take the "call me when you're really free" stand, get on with your life, and be happily surprised (or not) to hear from him a year or two later when he actually *does* call after he's free, hoping for a second chance. But if you bet on this actually happening, know that you are the kind of person who should never go near Las Vegas.

———

JUST DO IT. YOURSELF.

———

My salad days, when I was green in judgment.

—Shakespeare

More like *tossed* salad, those early days as a single parent. And my judgment was, indeed, very green. But on the upside, so was the lawn.

These were manic years, when I tackled every home improvement and repair personally out of fear that if I didn't, my kids would think something was missing (i.e. a father). This is what happens when you've been married for more than a decade to a man who mows the lawn diagonally, in both directions, no less, and then you get a divorce and labor under the insane delusion that you must wield a weed-whacker with the best of them or you're a complete failure.

The hundred-year-old Victorian home I had purchased in New Jersey gave me plenty of opportunities to indulge this obsession. The house was charming, historic, and quaint. Which, for those who have never spent hours poring over the Renovators Supply Catalogue, is realtor-speak for "eats money." No matter what went wrong, whether it was a rotting column on the front porch or a broken old window, the answer from suppliers was always the same: "They don't make 'em like that anymore!" They usually intended this as a sort of compliment, a tip of the hard hat to more elegant times in the construction biz, but simply translated, it meant one thing: that your treasure of a home would cost a small treasure to maintain.

And so, I could always rationalize my do-it-yourself compulsion on an economic basis, even if my true motives were psychological and extremely muddled. Looking back on it now, I see it all boiled down to one unconscious phrase: "I'll show them!" I'm still not sure who "them" was, other than my ex-husband, who could have cared less, or my children, who were unimpressed. At least, I never overheard them bragging to their friends, "*My* Mom knows her AC from her DC. You betcha!" Not that these years were wasted. No, in the time it took to evolve from "showing them" to "hiring them," I learned plenty. Everywhere I turned, in fact, there was another chance for Personal Growth.

The old swimming pool in the backyard, for instance, provided me with all sorts of insights: a new appreciation for subjects I had pretty much ignored in high school science (specifically, pH balance and the staying power of algae); the thrill of checking the skimmer basket for corpses of critters that made the mistake of going for a late-night swim (skunks were regulars); and a lesson in what can happen when a young lad at a birthday party decides to stop up the nozzle that allows water pumped from the filter to flow into the pool (the explosion of the cholorinator, a toxic cloud of chlorine, panicked evacuation of all celebrants, and a barrage of foul language that no doubt traumatized the boy in question to the point that he probably never wet a toe in a pool again).

The tall shrubbery surrounding the pool, which had been carefully shaped over the decades into perfect ovals and rectangles, provided me with the chance to take my new electric hedge trimmer up on the top stair of my new aluminum stepladder and, in one desperate, wild lunge after another, try to maintain the status quo. Either the previous caretakers had been much taller or the shrubs much shorter, but the net result was a row of bushes with a slightly lobotomized look. The last owner had left behind some equally grotesque garden gnomes, which I decided to leave in place, giving the backyard a sort of *Alice in Wonderland* ambience that would, no doubt, give Martha Stewart fits but thrill the Mad Hatter. I also mowed the lawn, until it finally dawned on me that other busy people usually hired someone to do this for them.

Even so, I must admit I enjoyed the do-it-yourself years. I liked pushing my Sears Toro up and down, back and forth, in a sort of walking meditation, the incense of freshly mowed grass and wild onions wafting over the whole Zen experience. Long after I'd hired a guy to take care of the lawn, I'd catch myself staring wistfully out the window as he buzzed by, feeling somewhat cheated, like the fellow chopping wood in that Frost poem who was approached by two tramps looking for work, just at "the time when most I loved my task," handing it over reluctantly, despite the logic.

The truth is, the physical chores of home can be a terrific antidote to the cerebral chores of work.

Unless, that is, the chore involves vermin.

I speak here not of the bats that would occasionally fly down the chimney. No, they were netted easily enough and returned to the sleepy suburban night.

And I speak not of the carpenter ants I found under my old wooden porch. Sure, I was concerned at first. But then an exterminator assured me, "Not to worry. These guys work very slowly." Were they union ants, I wondered, toting little lunch pails and taking lots of coffee breaks? And how did he know when they'd first punched in? No matter, I decided to take his word for it and postpone that particular battle.

No, I speak not of bats, nor ants.

I speak of squirrels.

Now, if you live in the city and your only acquaintance with the family *Sciuridae* is a furry flash of fluff scampering through the park, you may take offense at the characterization of squirrels as vermin. You may think they are adorable little creatures that are concerned only with storing nuts for the winter.

They've got nuts, all right. For make no mistake: Squirrels are rats in cute costumes. They are cunning. Machiavellian, even. They are, in short, the Enemy. I know this because I spent the better part of a year waging what became known in our family as "The Squirrel Wars."

It all began with Hitchcockian foreboding; just a few at first, then more and more, gathering every afternoon on my back porch. I suppose, in retrospect, I provoked the uprising by first providing a tempting treat and then trying to foil any efforts they made to reach it. The treat, of course, was birdseed, placed in a feeder described by the manufacturer as "squirrel-proof." I'm still grimly amused when I see variations on this concept advertised in gardening catalogs. As though any mere mortal, L.L. Bean included, could actually outwit a determined squirrel.

Squirrels are among nature's most agile acrobats. If they weren't so annoying, they'd be admirable. Leaping from a tall tree in a single bound, they can reach any bird feeder from any distance, grab hold with a death grip, ride out the swaying motion of the crash landing, and clamber into the feeding tray, even

if it means hanging upside down from the squirrel-proof roof. I
tried everything I could think of to foil their efforts, from barbed
wire to Vaseline. Nada. A couple of squirrels even began taunting me, hopping up on the window ledge at bird-feeding time,
fixing me with an impatient stare. I began shouting at them and
muttering to myself—never a healthy sign.

The battle was joined.

If they had been content to hold the line at the bird feeder,
perhaps the conflict would not have escalated beyond a little
backyard brawl. But one Saturday morning, they staged a predawn raid (is there any other kind?). At about 5 A.M., I was awakened by the obvious sounds of squirrel sex, coming from inside
the walls of my very own bedroom in the converted attic. Now,
you may be thinking, "What *are* the obvious sounds of squirrel
sex?" Believe me, you'd know it if you heard it, especially if you
were lying (alone!) in your bed on one of the few mornings you
could sleep past 3:00. And it wasn't the last time they would
taunt me with their huffing and puffing, squirming and squeal-
ing. After awhile, when the pungent aroma of squirrel urine
began to permeate the boudoir, it became clear that they had
moved in, and set up camp right under my sensitive nose, within
earshot of my sensitive libido.

This then, was war.

I called for reinforcements. An exterminator located the hole
they'd chewed through in the wood on the outside of the house,
and deduced that they were using my elegant old dogwood tree
to climb up on the roof. "You've got a choice," he said grimly,
"You can try to drive them out, which will be very difficult, or
you can solve the whole problem with one fell swoop, literally,
by cutting down the tree."

Cutting down the tree, I responded huffily, would be tanta-mount to surrender. He shook his head, but didn't argue. He'd no doubt seen that crazed look in many a homeowner's eye and knew it was futile to debate the issue. And so we devised a bat-tle plan.

One Saturday afternoon, when we figured our furry foes were out doing their nut thing, the exterminator pumped enough toxic chemicals into the house to kill everything that moved. As the kids and I stood on the street outside, we wit-nessed a wondrous exodus of creatures that shared our residence. They scurried and scuttled and winged their way to safety, as the house underwent insect exorcism. No sign of the squirrels, so we felt it was safe to assume they were out for the day.

Quickly, we implemented our second stage of attack. A car-penter I'd hired just for this occasion hurried up a ladder and nailed sheet metal over the hole the squirrels had been using as a door to their new digs. "That oughta do it," he said when he came back down. "Nothing could chew through that." The ex-terminator, veteran of many a squirrel skirmish, gave him an ominous smile. "Well," he said, "we can hope."

That night, all night, the ousted enemy sat on the roof and screamed. It's hard to describe a squirrel scream, but suffice it to say, cougars can't begin to compete. They were clearly pissed. What's more, they were clearly determined. By the next morn-ing, they had once again breached the perimeter. I raced outside to see how. There, next to the sheet metal, was a brand new hole.

Now, it was personal.

I marched down to my local hardware store, a place where you could still buy one nail at a time, a place where the clerks could talk you through the most intricate rewiring job, a place with aromatic wooden floors that evoked memories of the Tum-A-Lum Lumber Company, a place where they knew, as I did, that squirrels were no better than Skaggits.

"What's the best way to trap squirrels?" I asked the high priests of do-it-yourself.

"The Have-A-Heart Trap. Without a doubt."

"I don't want to have a heart," I said.

"That just means the trap won't kill 'em. It allows you to re-lease 'em somewhere far, far away."

At that point, a woman who had been listening to all this leaned over and whispered, "You know, you don't *have* to release them. You can do what I did."

She had that crazed look I'd seen in the mirror too many times.

"Oh, and what's that?"

"You just cover the trap with a blanket, run a hose from your car exhaust to the trap and . . ."

"I don't think I'm ready for that," I said hurriedly, "but thanks anyway."

Clearly, this squirrel thing had pushed more than one person over the edge.

I set the Have-A-Heart under the dogwood tree, baited it with Skippy peanut butter (I recommend chunky), and waited. It's hard to describe the frisson of joy that rushed through me with the capture of my first POW. He, on the other hand, was frantic, clawing at the bars with his tenacious little claws. But I forced myself to remain cool and detached by concentrating on all those mornings I'd been subjected to their cruel tortures. I placed the trap in the car and drove across town to the park. I re-leased him in a grove of enormous trees, an act of real charity, I thought, considering that I'd been tempted to release him on the New Jersey Turnpike. Of course, he was separated from his extended family. But not for long.

Over the next few months, I captured and relocated more than thirty squirrels. I knew things were getting a little out of hand when, on Christmas morning, I hurried past the kids as they rushed downstairs to open their gifts, raced to the window, threw open the sash, when what to my wondering eyes did appear, *yes,* another squirrel in the trap!

"Got one!" I screamed.

"Mom," said Kristen, exchanging a worried glance with her sister, "don't you think this has gone too far?"

"Too far? Too *far?* But I haven't trapped them all yet!"

"Maybe you're just picking up some neighborhood squirrels at this point. Maybe they were just passing through. How do you know they're the same ones that were living in the attic?" she asked.

She had a point. I hadn't heard a squeak out of our resident rodents for weeks. In fact, once I put my mind to it, I realized I hadn't been seeing many squirrels of any kind in the entire neighborhood. Perhaps I was, in fact, guilty of "collateral damage." And so, on Christmas Day, I declared peace, put away the old Have-A-Heart, unilaterally declared victory, and retired from the squirrel wars. Not that I still don't flinch when one scampers across my path. And the experience may have had a lasting professional impact. I'd like to think it made me much wiser when confronted with the sort of sentimental anthropormorphism I encounter so often in the news business.

Like the time, years later, when I was assigned to do a TV news story about the federal government's program to help sheep and cattle ranchers kill predators. While I was interviewing a rancher in Montana about all the lambs he was losing to coyotes, he said, "You know, they're just big rats in cute costumes." Naturally, we bonded.

After my producer and I had edited what we felt was an extremely balanced story and sent it back to New York, my then-editor called and said, in a disappointed voice, "I don't think you captured the beauty of this animal."

"Which one," I asked, "the lamb or the coyote?"

"The coyote, of course," she sniffed.

"I thought the debate here was not whether one animal had more rights than another but whether the taxpayer should be subsidizing the ranchers' war against predators."

"Well, it just won't work unless we can feel something for the coyote, and the piece just doesn't help us do that. Maybe some slow-motion of a coyote running through a field?"

The piece never aired. Not that it mattered, one way or the other. The coyote is thriving. So, too, is the squirrel.

If my confrontations with critters were crazy, my forays into matters mechanical were downright maniacal. Of the many memorable dramas in this arena, The Assembly of the Gas Grill stands out. It begins in the familiar way: You spot a really spiffy barbecue grill in the store, purchase it, and are handed an enormous box with all pertinent parts and instructions. At least, that's what they tell you. "A ten-year-old could put this together!" says the salesman, reassuringly. Unfortunately, the ten-year-old wasn't included in the price.

Days later, with the garage floor covered with strange parts that didn't seem to match anything in the instructions, something faintly resembling the thing in the store began to take shape. Finally, after much sweating and swearing, we were ready for the inaugural lighting ceremony in the backyard far, far, far from the house, which, for all I knew, was not insured for propane gas explosions. My children were ordered to stay inside, under cover. My Significant Other at that time, a Brit who found himself torn between native instincts of caution and gallantry, erred on the side of the obvious and managed to find a reason to be busy elsewhere. It was a lonely launching, but, other than a rather frightening initial flareup, a successful one. We cheered, we grilled, we ate. All summer long, in fact. It was not until the following spring, when I uncovered my proud achievement for a second season of glory, that the trouble started.

After turning on the propane and firing up the grill, I went inside the house to get the hamburgers. Moments later, I returned to see a Dali-esque disaster. All the dials on the front console had melted and dripped down to the ground. I managed to turn off what was left of them, and the gas, without injury. Except, of course, to my ego. Where had I gone wrong?

I went inside and found the instruction manual in the kitchen drawer reserved for these sorts of books, the ones we should read ahead of time but never do. Here is what it said, and I am not making this up: "If you have trouble starting the grill after a period of disuse, you may have cobwebs in your orifice."

I found this, metaphorically speaking, a bit over the top. Things weren't *that* bad, I thought to myself. At any rate, I wrote to the company, asking for help with the requisite repairs. Today, folks probably just log on to some Web site (and how appropriate would *that* be): *www.web.orifice.org* or something of the kind. In the end, however, my masterpiece proved beyond repair and had to be scrapped. I went out and bought a simple hibachi.

Both of us went on to enjoy a cobweb-free summer.

I'd love to say that what I may have lacked in mechanical skills, I made up for in culinary skills. But that would be a lie. My mother, who ruled her kitchen with an iron (nonstick Teflon) hand, never brooked any interference in that domain and so I pretty much avoided the whole cooking arena. Sure, I served my own kids dinner every night, but Sloppy Joes and meat loaf hardly qualify as cuisine. Then again, my Mom's cooking was fairly pedestrian, as well, even if I never realized it at the time. Years later, after she had died, I found her old *Joy of Cooking,* spattered with gravy stains and bacon grease. The updated version of this cookbook had just been published, and I was struck by the disparities.

Thumbing through that old cookbook took me back to the meals of my childhood, complete with Jell-O mold salads and casseroles made with cream of mushroom soup topped, perhaps, with a dollop of Miracle Whip. My mother's cooking, in other words, was classic middle-American fare for those times: artery-clogging, lard-laden, and totally free of any ethnic influences that might threaten to spice things up.

But the old *Joy of Cooking* showed me that while my Mom's cooking may have been bland, perhaps even life-threatening, it was also very much in the mainstream. In the vegetable chapter, for example, original author Irma Rombauer offers this recipe for canned lima bean casserole, something she calls a "fine main dish."

"To the lima beans, add six frankfurters, sliced, cover with bread crumbs and cheese." In my house, that would have been Velveeta.

The new *Joy of Cooking,* on the other hand, was amended by

much trendier folk. One of the authors sums up the new version as "easy contemporary, ethnic, low fat, and fresh mushrooms, *not* canned mushroom soup." Its contents were dictated, in part, by focus groups, those ubiquitous but invisible committees who are gaining more and more control over our lives, from the news we watch to the noshes we eat. I suppose it's all in the name of progress, but I'm holding on to my old *Joy of Cooking,* just in case the tide turns again.

Not that it really matters in my family. None of us has shown a real flair so far for any sort of cooking, trendy or otherwise. I knew this tradition was safe when my oldest daughter called recently with a culinary question. She said she'd been asked to bring a dish to a baby shower, a dish with a name she didn't recognize.

"What's it called?" I asked.

"It sounded," she said, "like a platter of *coup d'état.* "

"Hmmmmm," I pondered, "could it have been a platter of crudités?"

"That's *it,* " she said, adding, "so what *are* crudités?"

"Easy," I said, "just raw vegetables served with a dip. You know, like Miracle Whip."

In other words, it's safe to say that my home cooking would never get me named Mother of the Year.

Which is why we were all a bit puzzled when, in fact, I *was* named Mother of the Year. While I was still anchoring *First Line Report* at CBS Radio, someone called from the National Mother's Day Committee, a group that apparently exists in order to raise money for worthy causes like the Foundling Hospital. The man on the phone told me I was one of several women from different fields (entertainment, business, politics, broadcasting) selected

as Mothers of the Year, to be honored at a luncheon at the Wal-
dorf—$100 a plate, a thousand a table. All those commentaries
quoting my reluctant offspring apparently had paid off.

"What a nice thing," I thought.

"What are they *thinking?*" said my oldest daughter. "How do
they know you're a good mother? Have they sent an investigative
team?" (This daughter would one day end up working at *60
Minutes.*)

"Are they aware that you often send out for pizza?" the
younger one chimed in. "That you're the *only* Brownie leader
who doesn't know how to make Thanksgiving turkeys out of
pinecones and pipe cleaners?" (This would be the future artist
speaking.)

And, almost in unison, "Do they know about the *Squirrels?*"

This was not exactly the response I was expecting. But once
they learned that they, too, could attend the luncheon, sitting up
on the dais by my side, they put a lid on their skepticism. At least
publicly. At home, the weeks before the Big Day were filled with
not-so-subtle hints of blackmail, punctuated by remarks like, "I
don't know, Mom. I would *think* a Mother of the Year would
have *time* to drive her kid to the mall. But hey, what do I know?"

But I won back all those points at the event itself when they
turned out to be among the *few* kids in attendance. As they sat by
my side, beaming, fellow honoree Ivana Trump (still married to
The Donald) turned to me and said, "Vot a goot idea, to invite
your *children!*" She may have filled more tables, by golly, but I'd
brought along the *proof.*

While it's easy to laugh now about those years of do-it-
yourself and I'll-show-them, I have to admit there were plenty
of times when I grew weary of shouldering all the responsibil-

ity, times when I wished some big strong cowboy would just ride on up to the old homestead, Shane-like, grab that spanner wrench out of my hand, and say, in a thoroughly sexist but sexy voice, "Let me do that, little lady. Don't you go hurtin' those purity little hands."

Times like the Saturday morning when I was awakened by the breathing of two kids and an asthmatic dog standing by my bed, prompting me to open one eye and one ear to hear, "Mommy, it's raining in the dining room." And wondering, in that moment, if I should have stayed married after all. Then realizing, *nah,* I'd *still* be the one who'd be getting up.

Even so, I keep an eye out for that cowboy.

CHAPTER
6

THE MOVE
TO TELEVISION:
A SOBERING
EXPERIENCE

Evil Angel, on my shoulder
Boy, you sure do know your stuff
First you start 'em with a little
'Til they just can't get enough.

—Jesse Winchester

Perfectionism runs in my family. So does alcoholism. This is what's known as a lethal combination.

When you're trying to be both parent and pundit, hard-headed journalist and soft-hearted lover, mower of lawns and cultivator of sources, good listener at home and tough interviewer at work, and, every now and then, a thrower of really good dinner parties because, by God, that's what *your* mother did and even though she had nowhere near the same pressures, your mother was, in fact, the mother of all perfectionists and serves as the standard by which your inner judge is measuring your every move, and when you repeatedly believe that you are failing to meet this impossibly high standard you've set for yourself, here's what happens.

You take a drink.

It takes the edge off. Well, not *off,* exactly. Beveled, is more like it. And if you've inherited the family's alcoholic genes (it skipped my parents, but the family tree is in near-collapse from the collective weight of addictive behaviors), then you take another.

And another. Until one day, you wake up and wonder where you left the car. Which is to say, you really Wake Up, in the true Buddhist sense of that term. And if you're really, really lucky, you still have a job and kids who love you and your health and, yes, your car.

I was lucky.

After years and years of knocking them back, I got knocked off my feet. Until then, I was what is known (usually by those still in denial) as a "functioning alcoholic." Which means that my drinking was usually limited to those times of day when I didn't have to deal with deadlines or daughters. Radio is a perfect career for this stage of the disease. Off the air by noon, a long liquid lunch, home to greet the kids, make dinner (with a couple of glasses of wine while cooking and eating), an evening of getting beveled, then off to bed, ready to start all over again at 3 A.M. the next day.

Of course, there were plenty of hints that "functioning" was a relative term. Like the time, late one night, when I was rushing home from a social evening to meet the babysitter's deadline and tore off the left rearview mirror when I hit a sign that said "keep right." Perhaps if it had said "keep sober," I'd have paid more attention. But then again, probably not, because there's nothing that will take the fun out of your drinking faster than admitting you've got a problem. That's why no one admits it until they have no choice.

And I mean *no* choice—No-exit, that's-all-she-wrote, end-of-the-line despair and demoralization. There are any number of signposts, in addition to the ones that actually damage your car, to tell you that you've hit this particular dead end, known in rehab circles as "your bottom":

- When you get up in the morning convinced that you surely must have the ebola virus, and a touch of alcohol in your coffee seems to make good medical sense;

- When you promise yourself that just for this day, you won't take a drink, and by 5 P.M. you're breaking that promise, heading to yet another liquor store to buy a really fine bottle of wine because, you tell yourself, it if costs a lot, you couldn't possibly have a problem;

- When you try to "moderate" your drinking by imbibing only on the weekends, and then find yourself looking forward to Friday night with an inordinate amount of enthusiasm that has absolutely nothing to do with the guy you might happen to be going out with;

- When you coerce an entire group into leaving a restaurant upon learning that it's in a "dry" county and driving fifty miles to get to the next one, even though everyone in the car is dying of hunger;

- When you tell yourself, "I can quit anytime," but never get around to doing it;

- When your children start saying things like, "Mom, you told us that *last night!*";

- When you're routinely making apologetic phone calls, as in, "I'm really sorry I told your houseguest he's a jerk. Oh? I said 'asshole'? Well, then, I'm really, *really* sorry.";

- When you look in the refrigerator the morning after your dinner party and realize you forgot to serve a main course;

- When you order two glasses of wine the moment you sit down at a restaurant because you can't count on the waitress returning in time for a second round, which occurs approximately one nanosecond after the first;

- When you feel so terrible about yourself and the things you say and do while under the influence that there's only one way to feel better and that way, you tell yourself, is to take a drink.

Then, and only then, you might ask for help.

Meanwhile, you hold on to that drink for dear life, even though it could eventually cost you your dear life. Because the *thought* of life without a drink is, well, unthinkable. This is why the motto "One Day At A Time" is so popular with recovering alcoholics. It takes *"never ever again"* out of the equation, breaks it down into something people who crave immediate gratification can readily understand: Success measured in terms of one little twenty-four-hour period. Don't worry about tomorrow, it says. *Now this!* is all that counts.

What might seem like a cliché to the general population is also, to alcoholics, an ever-present warning that this is one hell of a sneaky disease, one that can tap you on the shoulder at unexpected moments and whisper, "Aw, come *on,* you were never *that* bad," a disease that can seduce people who haven't had a drink for years, haven't even *wanted* a drink for years, with one single moment of enticement. Perhaps it's just the glint of the sun on a chilled glass of Chardonnay that winks at you as it passes by on a waiter's tray. Problem is, if you let the beast out in that single unconscious moment, you will soon learn (so the scientists and anecdotal evidence tell us) that it has been quietly gathering strength during its forced hibernation. And it will pounce with a ferocity it never had before, one cranky cougar on a bender.

That ferocity and the vigilance required to keep it at bay is one reason why many recovering alcoholics remain anonymous; who needs people warily wondering if you're going to be devoured at any moment? The other reason is prejudice; there are plenty of folks out there who still think alcoholism is a moral problem, not a physical one. Even the most well-meaning people, upon hearing that you're a sober alcoholic, will say, "Good for you! What willpower!"

It is, in fact, just the opposite.

It is giving up the egocentric idea that you can beat the disease with sheer willpower and, instead, accepting the humbling fact that you can't do it alone. You may be able to stay "dry" alone, which is basically when you are free of alcohol, but not free of thinking about it. Almost all of the time, actually. Which, as you might guess, can render the "dry" person into a fairly tense, humorless, tightly wound human being. "Sober," on the other hand, connotes a freedom of both body and mind, when the obsession to drink is lifted. This requires a cry for help, one that starts at gut-level, where despair dwells, and then finally works its way to the surface with an admission that, alone, you are no match for this creature that is stalking you.

Coming from a long line of perfectionists, this was not an easy concept for me to swallow, especially since I'd been able to hold it together for so long, exercising a white-knuckled version of willpower. Which is to say, as long as I could count on the regular routine of my radio schedule, I could schedule my drinking as well.

Then came television.

When ABC News came calling in 1990, I was definitely ready for a change. I just hadn't anticipated this one. "We like your work on the radio," said the voice on the phone, "and we were wondering if you'd like to try TV." It was flattering, but a little frightening. I had never expected to start a whole new career at the age of forty-three in a whole new medium, especially one that so clearly favored youth and beauty. I'd already heard myself referred to as a "veteran correspondent" which, in broadcast-speak, means "a good nose for news but a bit long in the tooth." That, and the fact that CBS pretty much regarded radio as the ghetto of the news division, had pretty much convinced me to give up the idea of switching to television.

So the ABC offer came as a tempting surprise. But it came with a hitch: I would have to move to Los Angeles, where the network was in need of another correspondent to cover the West. My daughters were heading into their junior and senior years of high school and I felt we had to make the decision as a family.

"Let me get this straight," said Kerry. "We'd be moving from New Jersey to Southern California. And this is a problem?"

But her older sister saw it as an enormous problem. Kristen was to be student body president in her senior year, and captain of the soccer team. I gave her the option of staying behind to finish high school and live with a friend, all the while praying that she wouldn't take me up on it. At the same time, I had my own guilt to deal with. As the daughter of a naval officer, I had attended three different high schools, from Hawaii to California to Virginia. I had hoped to give my own kids the continuity I'd never known, especially since they'd already suffered through a divorce and custody battle. And here I was, asking them to leave at such a critical time, just for my career.

I will always be grateful to them for what I know was not an easy decision, despite Kerry's breezy assurances to the contrary. They both agreed that ABC was making an offer "we" couldn't refuse. Kristen decided, at the last possible minute, that she would make the move, as well. Later, she would write about that rather wrenching decision-making process as a theme for her college application essay, proudly carrying on the family storytelling tradition of transforming angst into art or, at the very least, anecdote.

And angst is just what it was.

We had exactly one month to make the decision, sell the house, find one to rent in California, enroll the kids in a new school, enroll me in a new job, pack, move, and unpack. This is what's known as "getting settled," a misnomer if there ever was one.

And it was just the shot of adrenalin and anxiety I needed to put the drinking right over the top.

Where once I had been able to schedule my imbibing around fairly regular work hours, I was now at the mercy of people who clearly did not grasp the concept. If a story broke late at night, you were expected to go cover it, an idea that did not jibe at all well with my drinking schedule. Add to the mix two traumatized teenagers trying to adjust to a new high school where half the kids were from very privileged homes and the other half were bused in from not-so-privileged homes and where my kids felt out of place with both. Every day, for the first couple of months, they would come home from school with tearful tales of woe. Sometimes Kristen would skip the tales of woe and head straight for the phone, where she would call the airlines and ask about ticket prices, one way, to Newark. She would jot down the information with an angry flourish, say she'd get back to them, and storm off to her room.

And I would drink. Much, much more than before. Years later, I heard a woman say she knew she was an alcoholic the day she "bought the funnel." I understood this immediately. To hide my drinking from my kids, I would top off the level of wine in the bottle in the refrigerator, using wine from another bottle. I dreaded recycling day, because of the shame of having the sanitation guys add up the not-so-subtle clues. The guilt over moving my kids away from their friends and everything that was familiar, coupled with my own fears about starting a new job in a new medium at a company where I knew absolutely no one, raised my own Ghosts of High School Past. Just trying to grasp the lingo of my new trade ("Did someone order a bird?") was just another version of having to learn yet another locker combination. Every dormant adolescent insecurity came roaring to the surface. I would be unmasked as a fraud, I thought, some rube from radio who doesn't know a satellite from a seagull. The psychologists call this "the imposter syndrome," an unrealistic fear of not measuring up. A good friend of mine calls it "getting in touch with his inner turd." No matter what you call it, it's bad news for the alcoholic.

Not long after we'd arrived in California, my bureau chief asked me if I would be able to go to Baghdad for a few weeks to be in place if the United States decided to go to war with Iraq.

I declined, pointing out that we had just moved and that I was, in fact, the only parent in the home, something she understood completely, adding that she just wanted to give me the opportunity. Even though I can't imagine having made any other decision, I was still riddled with self-doubt: Had I failed some important test? Should I have asked my parents to fly in to stay with the kids? Would I ever again be offered a major assignment like this? It didn't help that my oldest daughter thought I'd wimped out: *"Jeez,* Mom, the war with Iraq is going to be *the* story! What kind of reporter are you?"

A few weeks later, as we three were watching the news together at home, the broadcast switched to my colleague Gary Shephard in Baghdad. He was reporting live, as American planes attacked the Iraqi capital. Then, all of a sudden, he was cut off and the screen filled with static. And Kerry's eyes filled with tears.

"What's wrong, honey?"

"If that had been you," she said, "I don't know what I'd do."

That's when I knew I'd made the right decision.

But knowing I was right did nothing to ease my insecurity and fear. Only alcohol could do that, or so I thought. Problem was, it was no longer working its old magic. I was beginning to have blackouts, embarassing periods of memory loss. By this time, I knew I had a problem, that I couldn't quit, that it was getting worse. Thanks to my family history, I knew where that would take me: to a "bottom" much worse than the one I was in.

And the one I was in was bad enough. At the end of a long day at work, a day when I'd once again sworn to stop, a day when I'd stopped, all right, but only at another liquor store, I came home and started to cry. And then, I picked up the phone.

When I finally sought help, it wasn't hard to find.

I was referred to a meeting near my home. When I walked in, I was stunned; there must have been three hundred people in the room. From my vantage point, which was one of utter loneliness, it seemed as though half the town was in recovery. I don't remember much of what was said. It was enough to have reached out, to have admitted to the problem. The relief I felt that night in 1990 has never left me; I have not taken a drink since that time, at least as of this writing. One of the reasons this approach worked where everything else failed, I believe, has to do with the very nature of swapping empathic experiences, of understanding that, at last, "somebody else gets it."

Alcoholics tell great stories, sometimes gut-wrenchingly sad, sometimes riotously funny. I can't share them with you here, of course, because they are told in confidence, which is exactly why they are some of the most honest tales ever told. These are folks who have lived to tell the story and for whom telling the story is in itself a life-saving experience.

This is difficult to explain to normal people, people who take a drink or two and call it a night. I'm still amazed when I see someone in a restaurant get up at the end of a meal and leave behind half a glass of wine. "What's *that* about?" mutters the barely hibernating beast. "Why would someone *choose* to do that, to walk away from a drink when they don't have to?"

Because they *can* choose, of course.

As for recovering alcoholics, many of them choose to keep their dormant disease confidential. I gave up the comfortable cloak of anonymity when I was confronted with a different sort of choice. It happened at a GOP National Convention one summer, not too long after I'd gotten sober. I was among a group of women, including columnists, commentators, and correspondents, each extremely influential in her own medium, who had gathered to eat breakfast and swap stories. At some point in the conversation, someone started joking about twelve-step groups, and others joined in. This isn't hard to do; such groups are often the subjects of satire and parody, from movies to comedy clubs to late night television. Hell, I'd even done it myself.

But at that moment, I suddenly knew I had a choice to make. I could laugh along with them, much like a closeted gay person might do when the queer jokes start flying, or I could say something that might radically alter the way these very intelligent and influential women might think about the subject—and more importantly, the way they might write and report about it.

"I know these groups must seem silly," I said quietly, "with what you call their 'bumper-sticker philosophy.' And I'm certainly not the kind of person who gets caught up in new-agey, self-help, sentimental slop. But I'm here to tell you that these groups save millions of lives."

Silence. I plunged on.

"I know because one saved mine."

Their response was amazing. Glib repartee gave way to genuine remorse, followed by genuine interest. I've never regretted making the choice I made that morning. Or the choice I make every single morning, one day at a time.

This all sounds terribly serious, I suppose, in keeping with the connotation of the word "sober." But fortunately, sobriety and humor are not mutually exclusive. In fact, it is often humor that helps *keep* me sober. A shot of irony goes a long way, and there's no hangover.

A GREAT FACE
FOR RADIO

We All Want To Be Famous People and, the Moment
We Want To Be Something We Are No Longer Free.

—Krishnamurti

So true, so true. But then, Krishnamurti never had to work in television, a business that seems fairly oblivious to the Buddhist concept of ego-free living, a business that measures success with "Q" ratings, a quotient for gauging the *recognizability* of television anchors and, I suppose, any correspondent with enough visibility to create a blip on the radar screen of celebrity, meaning anyone who can get a good table at a restaurant. Radio people never get good tables, not even when they speak in stentorian tones meant to suggest "Hey, don't you *recognize this voice?*"

For reporters who start in print or radio, this emphasis on notoriety can be unsettling. In order to be an objective repository for other people's stories, journalists in those media learn to value the opposite of that ethic: that is, a low profile that allows the subject of the story to feel free to spill his guts to this innocuous, surely harmless, person he's speaking to. This is not to say, of course, that vanity does not play a part in print and radio. But it's generally limited to a byline or a sign-off. When television people talk about having a high "Q," which apparently has nothing to do with IQ, it often is used in conjunction with the phrase "the camera loves her."

I'd like to think that the camera has been known, on occasion, to *like* me, occasions like a perfect sunset, for example, that camera-kind time of day which has taught me to appreciate the vital link between good lighting and good journalism. And if the camera and I both happen to be in the same studio, one recently lit for, say, Diane Sawyer, we might even manage a one-night stand. But *love?* I don't think so.

So when a consultant who'd been hired by the network to help out new correspondents arrived from New York for a "session" with me, I was eager to hear what she might suggest. After years of coming to work dressed pretty much any way I wanted with a minimum of makeup, I had accepted the fact that *some* adjustments would be in order.

We sat down at a video screening machine and looked at some of my stories.

"Hmmmmm," she said after viewing a few. "I can see I don't have to help you with your writing or delivery."

"Hmmmmm," I thought to myself. *"Are* there correspondents hired by the network who *do* need help with their writing and delivery? And why would they be hired?" I had so much to learn.

"Well," I said, "what about my, um, 'look'?"

"Hmmmmm," she said, as she froze the video at one of my "standups," those fifteen seconds of fame when correspondents actually appear on screen in a story. She said nothing for what seemed a very long time, giving me ample opportunity to wonder how much she earns for one of these 'sessions.' "

"I really only have one word for you," she said finally.

"Oh? What's that?"

Then, like some character out of *The Graduate,* she leaned over and whispered in my ear.

"Scarves."

"Scarves?" I replied, as I mentally filed away "TV consultant" as a future career option.

"Yes, scarves. I think it would help soften your angular face."

In radio, I'd never had to worry about my angular face. In fact, I never realized I *had* an angular face. This was the first in what would become a series of insecurities about the "face" thing, something most television correspondents don't really like to talk about because it does, after all, smack of vanity and we're supposed to be in the business of telling *other people's stories.*

Even so, you begin to pick up enough hints, after awhile, that the "face" thing is *very* important to the people who hired you. Like the day I arrived at the bureau with a new, very short haircut, and the person on the newsdesk said, with a shocked expression, "Did you talk to *New York* before doing that?"

"I didn't know I *had* to," I answered, wondering just who in the hell you would call in New York to ask such a question. "Hey, Roone, whaddya say I go 'short' for a change?" Actually, I understand Roone Arledge *did* give that sort of personal attention to a number of correspondents he considered candidates for *"being something,"* as Krishnamurti would say. I was clearly not one of them, as evidenced by the fact that whenever I ran into Arledge in those early years, I had to be introduced each time.

At any rate, that visit from the consultant was pretty much it for outside help. And despite her advice, I've never managed to get into scarves, much less figure out how to tie them. And anyway, it seemed to me that scarves might be somewhat inappropriate for certain kinds of stories. Catastrophes, for example, in which large numbers of people die. Or, for that matter, any story involving a good headwind. And so I remain, to this day, an accessory-challenged correspondent.

Not that my more accessory-competent colleagues haven't tried to help. A couple of years ago, I was sitting on the set of *20/20* with Barbara Walters to pretape our closing "chat" about a story I'd done for that show. This basically involved a couple of questions back and forth about the piece, lasting maybe two minutes, max. The first take was a little rough, so we decided to do another. But in that very brief moment between take one and two, a phalanx of people managed to swoop down on the set to touch up hair and makeup. Barbara's, that is.

Up until that moment, I hadn't given much thought to whether any hairs had strayed. No one on the set seemed to give it much thought, either. As these attendants fussed over Barbara on the other side of the anchor desk, it became clear that I was on my own here, an anxiety confirmed with the arrival of the Lint Lady, a woman armed with one of those little sticky roller devices which she proceeded to roll all over Barbara's exquisitely tailored suit.

Ask not for whom the Lint Lady rolls. She does not roll for thee.

As I nervously began to hunt down and kill any lint that might have dared to show itself on my off-the-rack number, Barbara said, "Just one thing before we do this again."

"Yes?" I said, thinking she was about to suggest a different tack for our Q-and-A.

"Your pearls."

"My pearls?"

"They're crooked."

I looked down to see that, horror of horrors, my pearls were indeed crooked, the *clasp actually showing,* a fashion faux pas to the max. I straightened the necklace and we went on to a successful take two.

Of course, anchors *have* to worry about such things. Barbara Walters did not get to where she is today with crooked pearls. No-sir-ee. I, for one, could not stand the pressure (well, maybe for a multi-million-dollar salary). At least reporters who toil in the field only have to worry about those brief "standups" in the stories they file.

The ostensible reason for shooting a standup is to explain something in the story where there is no appropriate video available to cover the words. At least, that's the theory. But any honest reporter will tell you that it's also his or her only chance to get a little "face" time, that fifteen seconds or so that violates everything that Krishnamurti stands for, but which might, with any luck, lead to that elusive life of "Good Table." I say "elusive," because almost a decade in this medium has taught me that fifteen seconds of face time once or twice a week does not lead to instant recognition in the street, much less preferential treatment in a restaurant.

Even so, correspondents get pretty wrapped up in those fifteen seconds. One former reporter at our bureau held something of a record for self-promotion in the standup category when he managed to put himself on camera for fifteen seconds in an obituary of a celebrity that ran only one minute in its entirety. Even in the competitive, self-promotional world of television news, putting your own face in someone else's obituary is still considered a somewhat tacky thing to do.

But outside of the obit, almost anything goes. In fact, "creative" standups are encouraged. And by creative, I mean any standup in which the correspondent does more than just stand there and relate information (a quaint concept). Just about the time I started in television, the oxymoronic "walking standup" was all the rage. It didn't matter if walking made any sense in terms of what was being said, it was just considered a device to keep the piece *moving* (in other words, to keep an MTV-nurtured audience *watching*, which, in fact, they probably aren't doing anyway). And so you began to see correspondents walking down stairs, through turnstiles, along a crowded street, gesturing and talking while passersby looked at them somewhat askance. These days, passersby *really* pass by, so common are these walk-and-talks in our media-saturated society. Ho-hum, just another reporter trying to walk and talk at the same time.

Today, a simple walk down the street barely qualifies as "creative." These days, Reporter Involvement, or R.I. as it's called, is *de rigueur.* And so you'll see correspondents giving their spiels while riding on roller coasters, driving cars, climbing trees, hot-air ballooning, magically inserted into 3-D video games, and other assorted tricks of the trade. I personally am guilty of at least three of the above, all of which worked quite well, I thought. On the downside, these "creative standups" are often the only thing people remember about the story.

"I saw your piece on the news the other day," a friend will say.

"Oh, which one?"

"I can't remember exactly, but you were standing inside a video game, which I thought was really cool."

When I first came to ABC, I was quite nervous about this whole standup thing, and tended to take any advice I got. A cameraman suggested that I stand with one shoulder back, turning my head just slightly to look into the camera. Perhaps, I thought, this makes the reporter look thinner. So, in keeping with the addictive reasoning of my brain circuitry which basically says, "Hey, if a little is good, a lot must be better," I kept right on putting that shoulder back until it was completely out of frame and my head was almost turning at a right angle to gaze, sultrily, into the lens. One day, after one of my stories had aired on *World News Tonight,* the executive producer, Paul Friedman, called me.

"Is there something wrong with your left shoulder?"

"No, why?"

"I'm just curious as to why we never get to see it anymore."

The next standup I did was a full-shouldered frontal assault worthy of a linebacker. Friedman called again.

"I'd like to welcome your left shoulder back to the broadcast," he said.

He called on only one other occasion about a standup. This was a story about crime, a rather straightforward piece laced with dry statistics. My cameraman that day was a freelancer who usually shoots for entertainment shows. He had suggested that I might like what he called his "Lauren Bacall" filter, basically a sheer black Christian Dior stocking (I gathered that the brand was a critical factor), stretched over the lens inside the camera. Sure, I said, what the hell.

Heaven, was more like it. The standup was beautiful, a soft–

focus close-up smack dab in the middle of this rather dull piece about crime, dissolving into frame like some sort of ephemeral vision. My face was soft and beautific, no angles, no wrinkles, no nothing. And no scarf required.

Friedman called.

"What was that?"

"What was what?"

"That *standup!*"

"Yeah. Really great, wasn't it?"

"Not unless you're going into the movie business. This is *news*. Reshoot it before the next feed."

Despite the fear that I might never look that good again, at least not under the blazing noonday sun, I found this response somewhat heartening, affirming that those in charge still drew a distinction between news and entertainment, even if that distinction, at least in this case, boiled down to A Filter Too Far.

Problem was, my ego had known the illicit thrill of sheer black Christian Dior. Like some convenience store thief who pulls pantyhose over his head to cheat the security camera, I began to wonder what it would be like to fool all of the cameras all of the time, to rob time on a regular basis. After all, here I was, in Los Angeles, home to hundreds of Time Bandits, otherwise known as plastic surgeons. Although I didn't pursue this larcenous line of thought for several years, the seed had been firmly planted.

Perhaps if I'd been posted to a bureau in, say, Beijing, the seed would never have sprouted. But here, people go to cosmetic surgeons with about as much frequency as they visit the dentist. Maybe more. When first we moved to L.A., the kids and I had a good chuckle or two over all the folks walking around with that deer-caught-in-the-headlight look that indicates A Facelift Too Far. But then I began noticing that a lot of people my age looked at least a decade younger. Sure, I'd spent a lot of hours on a surfboard when I was young, sans sunscreen. And sure, there were all those years of smoking and drinking. But I couldn't imagine sun and sin accounting for *that* much of a disparity. Then I realized: These were the people who got *good* facelifts. The seed began to germinate.

Still, I resisted, even when our family dermatologist suggested, somewhat offhandedly, that I might try Botox to get rid of those deep wrinkles, "worry-lines," I think he called them, between my eyebrows. Like the angular face thing, worry-lines were not something I'd given much thought to before. Now, I couldn't pass a window without noticing them in the reflection, two huge crevasses right between the eyes. Even so, the thought of someone injecting me (we're talking a needle in the face!) with a substance made of botulism (usually paired with the word "poisoning") did not make me an enthusiastic candidate for what is sometimes called the "lunch hour facelift." Apparently, Botox paralyzes the muscles in your forehead, making it *impossible* to frown. Personally, I've always found frowns to be an important part of my emotional repertoire, and did not feel like giving them up. Not only that, and here's the clincher, you have to get regular injections of Botox (a needle in the face!) every three months.

So no Botox. But as I neared my fiftieth birthday, I once again heard the time bandits calling to me. I called for an appointment with a Beverly Hills surgeon who was reputed to have "worked on" some famous Hollywood stars. "What could it hurt," I thought, "just to hear what he thinks?"

And so I sat in his waiting room, surrounded by nose jobs and eye jobs and boob jobs and God-knows-what jobs, feeling extremely out of place and ambivalent about the whole thing. Before I had made the appointment for the consultation (a three-month waiting list!), my daughters had tried to talk me out of it.

"How *could* you?" said Kerry, with a frown. "After all you've taught us about the importance of accepting yourself just as you are and the dignity of aging gracefully and all that stuff! Didn't you *mean* it?"

"Of course I meant it," I said. "But I said that when I was forty. Now that I'm almost fifty, I've learned a few things."

"*What* things?" demanded Kristen.

"That I'd rather look forty, for one. And that consistency is the hobgoblin of little minds, for another. Besides, I'm just going for a consultation. I haven't decided on anything yet."

Between their disapproval and my ambivalence, I was growing more and more uncomfortable in that waiting room and had just about decided to get up and leave when my name was called. I was ushered into the doctor's office, where he placed me under an unforgiving light and in front of an unforgiving mirror. He looked long and hard at my unforgiving face.

"*So,*" he said after what seemed forever. "I guess you're here about those jowls?"

Jowls? Richard Nixon had jowls. J. Edgar Hoover had jowls. *Jowls?*

Let me tell you, *jowls* is a marketable word. If the ghost of my mother had suddenly appeared before me in that moment and pleaded with me to leave my face alone, *jowls* would have exorcised her in a heartbeat. There is no ambivalence in the presence of the word *jowls.*

"Right. So, what needs to be done?"

He went on to explain how he would eliminate the jowls I never knew I had. I hastened to say I didn't want him to touch my eyes or my forehead, that I had grown fond of the various expressive lines that had taken root there. In other words, if I was going to "have work done," I didn't want to *look* as if I had had "work done." He agreed. In fact, he did such a good job of making me look pretty much the same, sans jowls of course, that I've sometimes wondered if I got my money's worth.

As for the kids, they finally settled down when they could see that, in fact, I looked pretty much the same. By that time, however, I had introduced a new ethos into our little vault of family values. "You have to do what's right for you," I had said, a self-serving statement that would boomerang years later when Kerry came home for a visit and announced, as we waited for her bags at the airport carousel, "I have something I need to tell you."

I hate conversations that start with, "I have something I need to tell you." The next sentence is never along the lines of, "I won the lottery." It is along the lines of, "I got a tattoo."

"Oh, *Kerry,* you *didn't!*"

"I knew you'd react that way."

"Where *is* this thing?"

"On my arm," she said, "but it's a really nice one. I designed it myself."

By this time, I was emitting sounds not dissimilar to the keening of deep grief.

"Jeez, Mom, it's not the end of the world."

"You don't understand," I wailed. "I gave birth to that arm. And everything attached to it!"

"Well," she said with a huff, "somewhere along the age of eighteen, it became *mine.*"

I had to admit, it was pretty much a quid pro quo. A tattoo for a tuck. If there is one value that does *not* change in our family, it is disdain for hypocrisy. And this was definitely checkmate.

Of course, some people might say that rejecting scarves while accepting scars could qualify as hypocrisy. My only defense is that, as words go, "scarves" has nowhere near the power of "jowls."

Not that *any* of this amounted to much when it came to upgrading my public persona. I remember walking into a bank about six months after I'd started working in TV news. As I signed my check to be cashed, the teller looked at the name and said, "Judy Muller?"

"Yes."

"Are you *the* Judy Muller? The one who . . ."

(Here it comes, I thought. Recognition at last!)

". . . who used to be on the radio? Whatever happened to you?"

Things have not really improved since then. Years later, I was sitting on a United Airlines flight, watching the packaged news show on the cabin screen, a show provided at that time by ABC. I hadn't realized they'd used one of my features, but there it was, complete with several Reporter-Involved Moments. The man next to me was watching, as well, and laughing heartily (a good thing, since it was supposed to be a humorous story). I couldn't resist a prideful moment. I turned to him after it was over, and said, "I'm glad to see you liked that."

He looked directly at my face, the *same face* that had just appeared on the screen in front of him, and said, somewhat puzzled, "Yeah, that was pretty funny." And then, without a glimmer of recognition, went back to watching the screen. This does not bode well for a high "Q."

The only times I have been recognized, in fact, were those times when I'd rather *not* be, thank you very much. This includes a scene in a Manhattan restaurant where my boyfriend and I were having one of those emotional, "Where Is This Relationship Going?" conversations. Just as I was losing the battle to fight back tears and had started to sniffle into my salad, the waiter approached and said, "We have a bet going in the kitchen. I say you *are* her. They say you're not."

I looked up at him, red-eyed and weepy, and sniffled, *"Who her?"*

"Judy What's-her-name. You know, the newswoman."

"Woodruff?" I offered, hopefully.

"No. The woman reporting on the Simpson trial for *Nightline.*"

"Right. That's me."

"I *knew* it," he said, and went racing back to the kitchen to collect his winnings.

And then there was the time aboard a plane when I realized I had left my reading material in the side pocket of my carry-on bag, which was stowed in the overhead. I got up to retrieve a magazine or two, completely forgetting that I had also packed some tampons in that same pocket. As I pulled out the magazines, about a dozen "o.b.'s" came raining down on the heads of the passengers, some of the little cylinders wedging in the seats, others rolling under God-knows-how-many feet. "What *was* that?" I heard one man ask, as an "o.b." rolled down the aisle. Just as I was trying to think of something clever to mask the moment, something along the lines of, "Now, who the hell put *those* up there" or *"Free samples* from Johnson and Johnson!" someone a few rows behind me said, in a fairly loud voice, "Isn't that Judy Muller, that TV reporter?" I slouched down in my seat, my ego once again in check, if not quite in Krishnamurti-land.

So good tables are likely to elude me to the end. The best I can hope for is to tag along now and then with folks who have accumulated much more "Q." Diane Sawyer, for one. When a few of us took her to lunch on one of her visits to L.A., I quickly grasped what an alternative universe that Q-place can be. We went to a local Italian restaurant, one we've all frequented countless times. Diane ordered a salad. When it arrived, I was astonished. "Is that the same salad I order all the time?" I asked the waiter. "The Chicken Caesar?"

"But of course," he said, with a sniff.

Perhaps the green-eyed monster was making things look not only greener, but bigger, but I could swear this salad was easily three times the size of the little number the rest of us had always been served. This salad was Olympian, Cosmic, Gigantic. I was immediately ashamed, of course, of my petty reaction. It reminded me of a day back at CBS Radio when my producer had been asked to work with Diane (who was at *60 Minutes* at that time) on a radio piece. She came back from this excursion to TV-land almost breathless with adoration.

"You know what's amazing about her?" she gushed.

"No, *what,*" I said, hearing the jealousy in my own voice.

"Not only is she pretty and smart and talented and rich, but she's also *nice!*"

"Well, of *course!*" I blurted. "How hard is *that?* It's when you're ugly and dumb and totally lacking in marketable skills and poor as a dog, *then* if you're nice, now that's *saying* something."

I had, of course, said way too much myself, exposing my TV-envy for all to see. Fact is, Diane really *is* nice. In fact, if I'd asked, I'll bet she would have shared that salad.

Meanwhile, ABC continues to appreciate good storytellers, hiring a large number of correspondents from print and radio. They may not be bound for celebrity, but that's just as well, because if there's one thing that can get in the way of a good story, it's the ego of the storyteller. And I guess I should be grateful for all the times I'm reminded of that. Like the day on *Good Morning America* when Charlie Gibson was interviewing Liz Trotta, a former female correspondent from CBS. She had just written a book in which she claimed *no* woman would be hired for TV news these days unless she's young and beautiful.

On the *contrary,* responded Charlie. Why, he knew of *several* women at ABC News who *clearly* weren't hired because "they were glamourpusses" but because they "have solid news credentials." And, he added, "None is the female equivalent of Stanley Stunning."

And then he proceeded to name us.

Poor Charlie. He really meant this as a compliment. After his remarks were reprinted in a couple of newspapers, and after some of us had called to say, "Hey, thanks for the compliment, but next time keep it to yourself," I'm sure he wished he'd never said anything at all.

In retrospect, I see his remarks were more complimentary than I knew at the time. Even the fellow who sat next to me on that plane was paying me a compliment, the compliment of laughter. He might not have recognized me, but he'll remember my words (well, for maybe an hour, anyway), which is, for a storyteller, the most important connection of all.

This is, I realize, a classic example of rationalizing. But I prefer to think of it as going with my strengths. For all my insecurities about the "face" thing, that little reporter in the brain rarely lets me down. When I had only been working in television news for a couple of months, I wrote a piece about urban trees. The producer I was working with is known for his creative visuals and unusual editing. After I'd written the script and tracked my voice to tape, he and the videotape editor proceeded to put the piece together. Then he called me in to look at the final product.

It was visually interesting, all right. The camera swirled as trees spun overhead. The camera panned up. The camera panned down. I was beginning to get nauseous.

"What do you think?" he asked proudly.

"Well," I said, "it's very interesting. But I think the pictures are a bit busy. I mean, they're so busy that we don't really listen to the words."

"Look, Judy," he said, getting a bit of an edge in his voice. "I know you've just come from radio, so you may not understand this."

"Understand what?" I responded, just as edgily.

"Television," he said in a patronizing tone, "is a *marriage* of words and pictures."

"Well, in *this marriage,*" I retorted, "the *words* are gonna be on *top!*"

He and I still have this argument on a regular basis, even though we remain good friends. But I still believe now what I believed then: that jowls or no jowls, scarves or no scarves, a reporter's best accessory is the string of words that, like so many pearls, can make for a beautiful story.

Just don't let the clasp show.

ETHICAL DILEMMAS IN A TABLOID AGE

———

Television is democracy at its ugliest.

— Paddy Chayefsky

W hen Chayefsky wrote the screenplay for *Network,* he envisioned a time in the future when network news would be driven entirely by ratings. A time when editors would no longer give people what they need to know, but rather what they *want* to know, as long as those people happen to belong to the right demographic group targeted by advertisers. *Imagine that!*

Network now seems like a quaint piece of historical film. In fact, it feels quaint even to raise the subject. Today, reality outpaces parody at warp speed. A friend of mine at CBS believes that Edward R. Murrow's documentary *Harvest of Shame* would never get air time today. After all, those poor migrant workers are hardly a prime demographic for advertisers. Today, it would probably be a magazine piece done by a consumer reporter, posing the frightening question: "Do you know who's picking *your* lettuce? Are they *clean?"*

But there are a few of us old dinosaurs who like to think there is still a line that separates the sleaze from the substance, even though it's increasingly hard to find in this post-Tonya-O. J.-

Monica era. From Buttafucco to Bobbit and beyond, slimy news has emerged from the primordial mud of the tabloids and climbed onto the front pages and evening newscasts of the mainstream media. *Why?* Because the people *want* it. This is not to say, of course, that *all* people want it, just the people who represent the target audience of mass consumerism, never a great barometer for taste.

Not that I'm an elitist on the subject. After all, I did cover both O. J. Simpson trials for *Nightline* and while we like to think we took the "high road," reporting only on what transpired in court, the "high road" is a fairly relative term when the low road is located somewhere between the Mariana Trench and the Continental Shelf. Even so, it was also a hell of a story, revealing sharp disparities between the way whites and blacks perceive the justice system (a revelation that was a surprise only to whites, by the way) and giving us a plot line so full of bizarre twists and turns that it would have been rejected if any screenwriter had pitched it ("So here's the concept: His blood is at the murder scene, their blood is in his car, but he gets off anyway . . .").

But stories of crime and sex and betrayal have always intrigued reporters, tabloid or not, so it's naïve to place the blame on ratings alone. The truth is, while the tabloid press covers what might be called "backyard fence journalism," that is, the stuff "everybody's talking about," the mainstream press wanders into that backyard not only because of ratings but because editors and reporters are human and like a good story as much as anyone. Given a choice of, say, NAFTA or Monica, which one would *you* choose? The very *word* "NAFTA" has a sedative effect, as in, "Take a NAFTA and sleep." Compared to an arresting word like "Buttafucco," "NAFTA" doesn't stand a chance.

On the other hand, hovering around the back fence for too long can warp our perspective. I remember going to Portland a few years back to do a story on Oregon's rather radical health care program and running into a mob of reporters in the hotel bar. This was during the time when Tonya Harding's attack on Nancy Kerrigan was the scandal-du-jour and hordes of journalists were in town to track down every lead in this Incredibly Important Skating Saga, one that asked the Incredibly Important Question, "Just how long can a really good cat fight distract us from boring stuff like crime and poverty?" (The answer, apparently: "as long as the ratings hold.")

A correspondent from another network spotted me as I walked into the bar and came over to ask what I was there for, since ABC already had several folks in place. "I'm doing a piece on health," I said. "Tonya's or Nancy's?" he asked, clearly worried that he might have missed something.

And, of course, he probably had.

Today, no one gives a damn about Tonya and Nancy, but the crisis in health care affects everyone, whether they watch *Jerry Springer* or *Nightline*. It may not be a sexy topic, but talented editors and reporters can still manage to make such issues come alive with the use of that all-time effective device, telling personal stories that are symptomatic of a larger problem.

Our problem is finding the space and time to tell those stories. With network news losing audience to cable and the Internet, there is an increasing tendency to hook viewers with "news they can use," meaning lifestyle pieces that were once relegated to women's magazines, such as "New Study Says You CAN Have Great Sex after Fifty!"—something that hardly comes as a news flash to the group in question.

I'm not suggesting that television news, at least the half-hour evening news variety, has ever promised more than a summary of the day's events, with perhaps a dollop of analysis. And it has always been a challenge, whether working in radio or TV, to write succinctly. As Thoreau once said, "Not that the story need be long, but it will take a long while to make it short." Which is to say, I can whip out a six-minute script for *Nightline* faster than a one-and-a-half minute script on the same subject for *World News Tonight*. Writing "short" is very, very tough. But when it's done well, under tremendous deadline pressure, it can also be very, very satisfying.

So TV reporters are used to delivering complicated subjects in a simple package. But even that small parcel is being downsized to make room for more of these special segments aimed at giving people "what they want." This squeeze of available time regularly leads to frustrated calls from correspondents in the field to editors in New York to beg for a few more seconds, just five or ten, in order to adequately report their story, one which might have been told in two minutes in the past but now must be related in about the time it takes to burp. "I need *more time*," must be the most commonly heard complaint from the field.

The tug-of-war over time is just as frustrating at the other end, of course, because they're trying to cram the day's news into less than twenty-five minutes (even less, if you consider the "lifestyle" segments that increasingly vie for time with so-called "hard" news), while dealing with aggressive (or, depending on your gender, "difficult") reporters, each demanding more time to tell his or her story.

I once had a conversation with an editor that summed up this mutual frustration in an incredibly concise way. I called him at the "rim," which is what we call the semicircular desk where the anchor and executive producer and editors for *World News Tonight* sit while going over scripts from the field, in order to clarify the focus of the story I was working on for that evening's broadcast. Those of us who report in the Pacific time zone have three hours less than our East Coast colleagues to prepare a day-of-air story (dubbed, appropriately, a "crash") and so we like to make sure early in the day just what the "rimsters" have in mind.

"I'd like to get your take," I said, "on just what this story's about."

"It's about a minute-thirty," he said, and hung up.

Executive producers at all three networks have tried to provide some shelter for more substantive stories by creating segments entitled, variously, "In Depth," "Eye on America," and "A Closer Look." But given the current market-driven trends, I fear a day when even these will feel like "A Cursory Look."

While some of the powers-to-be at network news are struggling to hold the line, *local* news has all but surrendered (there are exceptions, of course, but they are increasingly rare). Here in Los Angeles, not one station has a news bureau in Sacramento, the capital of one of the largest and most influential states in the nation. I asked a local political reporter why that was the case and he didn't even have to pause to think about it.

"State government is a ratings black hole," he said.

"But don't you feel some sort of obligation to report on what politicians are doing in the name of the people who elected them? Isn't that part of a news organization's responsibility? To inform?"

Even as I said it, I knew I sounded hopelessly pedantic, a fussy old fossil from another place and time. And I knew the answer, anyway. Without ratings, local news broadcasts lose advertising dollars. Without advertising dollars, news directors (who, to begin with, have the job security of a dictator in a banana republic in South America) lose their jobs. Which means most news directors, who have families to support like everyone else, will opt for the Ratings Thing over the Right Thing almost every time. The few who resist that pressure should be declared heroes. Or, at the least, journalists.

So the standard format for local news is usually a program chock full of crime (hence the phrase "if it bleeds, it leads"), occasional high-speed chases (I confess to having become addicted to these and so, clearly, am part of the problem), and many, many maudlin moments in which the anchors ad lib, ad nauseum. One of my favorite such moments occurred a few Christmasses ago, while I was watching one of our local news programs. The two anchors were from the usual Ken-and-Barbie mold that can be seen advertised on billboards across America, morphing into one another from Fresno to Philadelphia. They were chatting about a story involving a "tragic" incident at the annual Christmas Parade. All incidents, by the way, are "tragic." "Sort of sad" doesn't do much for the ratings.

It seems the hot, dry desert winds known as Santa Anas were blowing especially hard that day, wreaking havoc with Santa and his elves, who were following that hallowed Christian tradition of parachuting out of a plane and into the parade route.

"So *tragic*," said Barbie, "when that elf plowed right into the crowd."

"Thank *God*," said Ken, "that the poor little girl wasn't more seriously injured. She took quite a hit. I understand she's still in the hospital but *miraculously* may be home by tomorrow."

(Another staple in such stories is a tendency to see almost everything as a miracle. And always, always to thank God, who has a very high Q rating.)

"Yes, but you just know that elf must be feeling *terrible* about it."

To which Ken responded, and I am not making this up, "Well, Barbie, I'm sure it's a sad day for elves *everywhere.*"

Of course, it's easy to poke fun at local news. So easy, in fact, that it's tempting to devote a whole book to it. But that would be unfair, since network news certainly has its own share of maudlin moments. I'm thinking now of the deaths of JFK, Jr. and his wife, Carolyn Bessette, and her sister. The reporting by networks started out tastefully enough, in direct proportion to our shocked and sad reaction to the news. But it quickly degenerated into a weeklong wailing and gnashing of newsteeth, punctuated by the reporting of each successive sign (a floating suitcase, a medicine vial) confirming the obvious, i.e., that they were dead.

It seems we never know when to stop, but surely a good place would have been long before the exchange between a network correspondent and the Reverend Billy Graham, in which she asked him this existentially absurd question: "Reverend, can you please help us understand how God could do this to us?"

I couldn't believe it. Did she expect God to say, in a deep rumbling voice, *"Pilot error"?*

Perhaps we've marched so far into treacle territory that extrication is completely out of the question. This was brought home to me during a conversation with a young news intern with whom I was working. She had just finished transcribing a two-camera interview I'd done (meaning, both my face and the subject's could be seen on camera).

"You know what you do really well?" she said.

"No, what?" I responded, thinking she was about to compliment me on my interviewing skills.

"Well," she said, "you've really got that listening shot down."

"That's because I *am* listening," I said.

"Yeah, that's what I mean. You've really got it down, you really look sincere."

It unnerved me to think that the next generation of journalists would consider *acting* ability a major part of the job description. But that is, in fact, where we seem to have arrived. Obviously, a good camera presence has always been an asset for television reporters. But more and more, at least at the magazine shows, correspondents are increasingly valued more for that attribute than for their writing skills. During one of my forays into that magazine world, when I was reporting a story on a rare mental disorder, another correspondent came up to my desk, which was overflowing with notes and interview transcriptions, and asked me what I was doing.

"Just writing my piece," I said, wondering why it wasn't self-evident.

"Oh, no, no, no. You'll never last here if you try to actually write your pieces," he said.

"What do you mean?"

"You'll be too busy, working on six stories at once, to actually do the writing. Let the producers do that."

"Good writers, are they?"

"Some, yes. Some, no. But you can always re-write anything you don't like later. If you have the time, of course."

Since I was hired by ABC News for my writing skills and *not* for "the face thing" (which Charlie Gibson had already made quite clear to the world, thank you very much), I could see this would present an obstacle for any long-term career in the "magazine" format. Clearly the preferred methodology was to airdrop in for interviews and standups and then voice the script when it was presented to you later, the "look, ma, no hands" approach. For a hands-on storyteller, it sounded like hell.

There are still a number of good storytellers who manage to inject their own style into magazine pieces, correspondents such as Robert Krulwich, Sylvia Chase, Lynn Sherr, Bob Brown, Judd Rose, John Hockenberry, and Christiane Amanpour, along with a few others. But the pressure to fill a growing number of hours of prime-time magazine shows means more pressure on these same people to be, well, ubiquitous. And that can't be good, in the end, for the integrity of the story.

And if I'd needed confirmation of that, the Peter Arnett debacle at CNN pretty much hammered it home. When CNN had to retract a story about alleged use of nerve gas by Americans during the war in Southeast Asia, it revealed the wizard behind the curtain in a way the public had never seen before. Arnett, apparently without any embarrassment at the time, said that he had just been the "face" on the story and had not contributed a "single comma" to its writing. The producers, he said, had done all that. Now, there are producers who are very good at doing all that. Some of them, in fact, are among the best investigative reporters in the business. But few people had known, previous to this incident, how big a part they play in the actual reporting and writing of a story. The Arnett flap was all the more bizarre because this was a reporter who had made his reputation as a tough war correspondent, a journalist in the old-fashioned sense of the word, a guy *no one* would describe as "just another pretty face."

Ah, how wonderful to be a "face," to take all the credit and none of the blame. The producers who put that story together were fired, while Arnett was not. He was, however, shunned by CNN to the point where he finally left on his own accord. He had committed the ultimate sin of admitting that he was, in fact, just "the face," a bit of honesty that, while apparently not embarrassing to him, must have embarrassed his network, not to mention the burgeoning TV magazine industry in which this had become common practice.

Then again, maybe not.

As more and more magazine shows take to the air, the competitive pressure to "get the get," to land the big interview or sensational exclusive, will increase. And that means more and more pressure for the "talent," as journalists in television are often called, to make themselves available for as many "gets" as possible, leaving the nitty-gritty details of the actual writing to someone else. This is no doubt one of the things that worried Don Hewitt, executive producer of *60 Minutes,* when CBS decided to add a second edition of that program to its lineup. Hewitt expressed a concern that there might not be enough good *producers* out there to staff another show. Correspondents, he said, he could always find.

The "get the get" race leads to other dangerous practices, as well. It can put the subjects of stories in the driver's seat, allowing them to negotiate terms in exchange for an exclusive. As the second O. J. Simpson trial was winding down, there was incredible pressure to "get" key jurors from the previous trial. In the week leading up to the civil jury verdict, the networks (and local stations) all were vying to lock in the criminal trial jurors so they would be available to comment on whatever verdict came out of the civil proceeding. A booker told me that one former juror had demanded a limousine, and a suite at the Doubletree Hotel (which was across the street from the Santa Monica Courthouse) for her and four of her closest friends for a whole week, along with all expenses paid for food and drink. ABC did not grant her wish, but I wouldn't be surprised if *someone* did.

In fact, whenever a major story breaks, whether it's a sensational scandal or a school shooting, you can just bet that the flowers and gifts are on their way to the key players (i.e., victims) within minutes of the story hitting the wires. These bouquets and fruit baskets usually have a signed note from a celebrated anchorperson or correspondent promising that they and *they alone,* as opposed to everyone else sending flowers and fruit, will be sensitive and caring. Apparently the power of celebrity wins out every time over the fear of exploitation, even at a time of grief and mourning. ("Can you believe it? Katie Couric wants to talk to US!")

I know of one case in which two magazine shows from two different networks were competing for an exclusive on the same story, which involved a nasty, but sexually provocative, lawsuit. One of the shows managed to get the "Get" by promising the plaintiff that the *other* side would never be interviewed. This is so offensive to everything that fair and responsible journalism stands for, that it seemed hard to believe when I heard it. But then I learned that the *other* party in the lawsuit had signed a similar exclusive with *another* show. Perhaps the audience should be advised, in such cases, that the *"Rest* of the story," as Paul Harvey would say, could be heard at such and such a time on another network.

Just as Peter Arnett inadvertently pulled the curtain back to reveal the true "face" of magazine journalism, the public got a rare glimpse of how the race for the "get" operates during an incident stemming from the O. J. criminal trial. A juror had been dismissed (I can't even remember why), and while no one was supposed to know the names of jurors, every news organization immediately went to work to discover this woman's identity so that she could be interviewed. Somehow, everyone came up with the same name at about the same time (which should have been a clue, right there), along with an address in Los Angeles. I'd say no more than a few hours had gone by before her apartment building was surrounded by producers bearing gifts and various limos ready to bear *her* to various studios. News helicopters hovered overhead, while neighbors going in and out of the building were hammered with questions. Did they know the woman? Did they know she'd been on the O. J. jury? Finally after an hour of this breathless anticipation, much of it carried live on local news stations, a young woman came bicycling down the street, dressed in gym clothes.

"What's going on?" she asked, as she weaved her bike through the armada of satellite trucks.

"Oh, we're waiting to interview a juror from the O. J. trial who lives here," responded the reporter she happened to ask.

"What's the name?"

And when he told her, she laughed and said "That's me. But I never served on the O. J. case."

But as soon as she said "that's me," she was surrounded by the mob. One network producer actually shouted, in his best interrogator's voice, "Can you *prove* that you were *not* a juror? And could we see some ID?"

As it soon became clear that this was not only a case of mistaken identity but a classic case of herd journalism, the limos began to slink away like so many hearses laden with wilting flowers. But some of the reporters, determined to get *some* sort of get, interviewed her anyway about how she *felt* now that she had been touched (or at least ambushed) by the trial of the century. And at least one reporter, this one, filed a piece about the screw-up itself. Because, hey, from an ironist's point of view, that was a much better story than if she'd turned out to be the real thing. In fact, when the real thing did turn up, she had almost nothing to say.

Of course, poking fun at your own profession is risky. As long as you happen to be covering the same story, it's hard to remain above the fray. During Simpson's criminal trial, *World News Tonight* sent me down to the courthouse to do a story on the media circus surrounding the case. In a sort of Pirandello-like confrontation, I found myself both audience and unwitting actor in that circus.

A woman who worked for a now-defunct TV tabloid show called *Premier Story* would station herself and her camera crew outside the courthouse every day for the sole purpose of conducting ambush interviews on the sidewalk, asking obnoxious questions she never really expected the answer to.

"What was in that bag, Mr. Kardashian?"

During these outbursts, the camera was always on *her* and it never stopped rolling because she was, in fact, her own story. If it can be called journalism at all, it might be called "masturbatory journalism." The actual story—that is, the brutal murders of two people and the trial of the famous man accused of killing them—was mere backdrop for the performance of the reporter.

I decided she should be an element in *my* story about the

media circus outside the courthouse. As soon as my cameraman started shooting the scene, she turned on him, peppering him with questions. He looked flustered, so I came over to help. I asked her what she was doing, and we got into this bizarre exchange in which she explained that she was simply interviewing *us* to find out why we were interviewing *her.* And round and round it went until the very dim bulb in my head flickered to *on* and I "got" that I was her "get" for the day. Her camera had been rolling the whole time.

When I walked away, I was followed by a guy holding a camcorder who kept pushing himself on me, whispering questions into my ear, such as, "Why won't you talk to that lady, Judy? Are you hiding something? You can dish it out, but you can't take it?"

His camera was literally two inches from my face. I kept trying to walk away, with no success. So finally, in a fit of frustration, I whirled on him and asked him to leave me alone, only I didn't say, "Leave me alone." I said something more direct, in language I would not normally use in the vicinity of a camera. But what the hell, I figured, this was just one of those wackos who hang outside the courthouse with an amateur video camera.

Then my producer gave me the bad news. "I kept trying to *tell* you," she said, "but you weren't listening to me!"

"Tell me what?"

"That guy works for *Premier Story.* I've seen him out here before."

The Skaggits strike again.

And so, I found myself no longer an ironic observer of the media circus. I was in the center ring, and screaming obscenities to boot. I later learned that the same people had harrassed Jeff Greenfield the day before when he was doing a story for *Night-*

line. The two of us and our confrontations with their cameraman made up the entire bulk of their show for two nights running, complete with my expletive barely deleted (rerun several times, in slow motion, no less). Jeff had no expletives deleted because he had the good sense, in the first place, not to utter them.

When I realized I'd been had, I promptly called the rim in New York. "Um, I need to tell you something." And I related what I had said and to whom I had said it and that the whole thing would probably wind up on a tabloid magazine show that evening.

Peter Jennings just laughed and said, "I'm sure you were expressing the sentiments of a lot of us." The executive producer just shrugged it off with a "don't-worry-about-it."

Actually, I was more worried about my father's reaction if he should happen to tune into the show. I can count the times I've heard my father use bad language on one finger and no, not that finger, because I've never seen him do that, either. Not because he's an uptight moralist, but because he's just a really decent guy, an officer and a gentleman, as they say. It was safe to say he was not a big fan of the F-word.

He didn't see the show, but, as it turned out, he read about the exchange in a newspaper article, which he shared with me by phone.

"I want to read something to you. They talk about you in this article."

I gulped hard (do we ever stop craving parental approval?) and muttered, "Go ahead."

"It says: *'Premier Story* milked the artificial conflict with Greenfield into a full 30-minute show. The next night's show was devoted to a similar run-in with ABC's Judy Muller, a respected political reporter. Face to face with a cameraman from *Premier Story,* an angry Muller finally told him to 'F . . . OFF!' "

After he read this to me, there was silence. I was embarrassed.

"I'm sorry about that, Dad."

"Why are you sorry?"

"Excuse me?"

"I think it's very flattering. They called you 'a respected political reporter.' "

On a bad day at the circus, there's nothing like the filter of family.

But this incident served as a grim (well, grim may be a bit much, but at the least, icky) reminder that tabloid sleaze was crossing more and more often into good old mainstream muck. The problem is that, with this annoying little thing called the First Amendment, anyone can call himself a journalist and, sometimes, even get press credentials. While journalists like to think of themselves as professionals, there is no system in place for licensing or policing that system. Nor would most reporters want one. For starters, who could possibly be in charge of such an effort? We trust no one, least of all ourselves.

So it would appear that we are stuck in the muck of our own making. Perhaps the best line of defense is for newsrooms to encourage spirited debate on ethical issues as they arise, although sometimes even that can go too far, especially when it comes to matters of political correctness. And yes, of course, I have a story to illustrate this, or I wouldn't have used that tortured segué in the first place.

Some years ago, the Mattel Toy Company came under furious attack from teachers and feminists for making a talking Barbie doll which said, among other things, "Math class is *soooooo* hard!" This only served to reinforce the stereotype, said the critics, that little girls, by nature, struggle with mathematical concepts. *World News Tonight* saw this, as I did, as a somewhat humorous story. Of all the things to object to about Barbie, her struggle with math would seem to pale next to, say, those pointed feet permanently locked in the stiletto heel position or enormous breasts poised for liftoff. The story was, in short, a tempest in a D cup, a phrase I would have shamelessly used had I had the chance.

My producer, Robin Weiner, had just arrived at the L.A. bureau after years working at bureaus in Europe, where she had covered stories like the fall of the Berlin Wall. The Barbie scandal was one of her first assignments in the states (welcome home!). As I headed out to interview the woman who headed up the Barbie Division (a woman with so much Barbie-like hair that the cameraman had trouble fitting her in the frame), Robin headed to the nearest Toys "R" Us to find a Barbie that says, "Math class is *sooooooooo* hard!" This, in itself, proved to be pretty hard. With the manager of the store standing over her, saying "You will have to *buy* all of those, you know," she sat on the floor and proceeded to rip into packages, insert batteries, and push buttons, in the relentless pursuit of just one doll programmed to say this particular phrase (the difficulty in accomplishing this only served to remind us how truly silly the issue was, if, in fact, we needed any reminders). After she'd determined that a doll was a dud, she would toss it over her shoulder. The pile behind her began to mount.

Finally, *yes!* a math-challenged Barbie was located and she put in a call to me over at Mattel. *"Got one!"* she cried in a triumphant tone worthy of the squirrel wars. "Just one thing, even though I doubt it matters."

"What's that?"

"The only Barbie I could find who says this is a black doll."

"Black, white, brown, what difference does it make?" I said.

Quite a bit, as it turned out.

I called the Rim and told the editor I was working with at the time that we were in good shape, interview and doll in hand. "Just one thing," I said, echoing Robin's exact words to me, "even though I doubt it matters."

It did. My editor was aghast.

"We *can't* show a *black* doll saying, "Math class is sooooooo hard!"

"Why *not?*" I asked, sensing I was about to slip into "difficult" mode. "You mean it's okay if a *blonde* is stupid?"

"We just shouldn't introduce a racial element into this," he responded.

"But that's exactly what you *are* doing!"

The very PC that we had been about to lampoon had come back to bite us. When I suggested that we could take the *audio* from the black Barbie and edit it over the *video* of a blonde Barbie, you would have thought I'd suggested violating the most sacred of journalistic codes.

"We don't do that."

"But," I sputtered, *"these are dolls!"*

The piece never aired.

I guess, in retrospect, I'd rather have an editor who errs on the side of sensitivity than one who errs on the side of sensationalism. What I really want, of course, is an editor who almost always

sees things my way, which is probably the fantasy of every reporter in every medium who word-wrestles with editors on a
daily basis. It is a built-in checks-and-balances system, a healthy
and necessary one, I suspect, unless the balance tilts too far one
way. The one area where this seems to happen the most is that
vast chasm between Manhattan and The Rest of the Country.
My editors work (and often live) in New York City. Those of us
who grew up in, and report from, the West, sometimes find that
chasm alarmingly wide.

I was first introduced to that great divide when I was a reporter covering politics in Denver. Then-Governor Dick Lamm
told me about a New York radio reporter who had called to interview him on the phone about a devastating blizzard that had
hit the eastern plains of Colorado. He told her that the ranchers
were having an especially hard time of it.

"Oh? And why's that?" she asked.

"Well, because of the huge snow drifts, the only way they can
feed their cattle is by helicopter."

A pause on the other end of the line. And then: "So, how
many cows can you *get* on a helicopter?"

I had thought this to be a unique anecdote, until I found *myself* staring across the chasm of never-the-twain-shall-meet. The
story about the Montana sheep rancher and his coyote problem
was certainly one example of this disparity in sensibilities. Another was when I wrote a piece about an anti-litter campaign
called "Don't Mess With Texas" in which someone I interviewed
said, "We're aiming this campaign at Bubba, the guy who throws
beer cans out the window of his pickup truck."

Keep in mind that this story took place before Bill Clinton
ran for President and introduced the "bubba factor" into the na-

tional discourse. My editor (a woman who is no longer there, but whose editing skills I usually admired) called me in the bureau for the dreaded "script approval process," which usually involves two or three editors weighing in from New York, including the anchorman.

"We like this," she said, "with just one criticism."

"Oh, what's that?" I said, knowing that "one criticism" could be anything from "change 'litter' to 'trash' " to "put the last sentence first, the first sentence last and get rid of most of the middle."

Prepared as I was for almost anything, *this* criticism threw me.

"We took an informal poll here, and it was unanimous. No one here has ever heard of this word in your script, what is it, 'Bubba'?"

"You guys really ought to get out more often," I said.

Not a good move.

"Humor us," she said, without a trace of humor in her voice. "Just what does it mean?"

"Well, Molly Ivins has a number of definitions. But the one I like is: "You know you're a Bubba when, if your porch collapses, at least six dogs die."

Still no reaction.

I plunged on. "Don't you think it's somewhat self-evident in the context of the soundbite?"

Apparently not. The Bubba bite was history.

Perhaps a solution to this problem would be to add a few more people to the rim who get out of Manhattan on a regular basis, who leave the Big Apple for a place where Real Apples are grown, and listen to the cadences and the concerns of people who live in those places. My childhood affection for my hometown of Milton-Freewater may color my view on this subject, but I do know that, as a grown-up, I find big-city snobbery toward small-town America a most loathsome trait. Once in a while that snobbery creeps into the editorial process, prompting sweeping judgments about people and places. Say "Idaho" to a New Yorker and he will think "white supremacists." On the other hand, say "New Yorker" to an Idahoan and he will think something unprintable. Seems to me our job as journalists should be to knock down those stereotypes, and get to the real issues that connect us all.

In other words, in addition to the guys they've got there now (and they are, for the most part, guys), perhaps there could be more, dare I say it, diversity. Not just in terms of gender and race, but also in terms of geography.

Until then, the best way to get on the air from here in Los Angeles, at least during a slow news week, is to do yet another story about those "wacky Californians."

In California, everyone goes to a therapist,
is a therapist,
or is a therapist going to a therapist.

—TRUMAN CAPOTE

For all transplants to this state, which is almost everyone *in* this state, there comes a moment when you realize that you have, in fact, become a Californian. For me, that moment came when I was caught for speeding on my way home from my meditation class.

True, my lead foot may still have had that East Coast urgency, but my mind was Malibu-mellow. I knew this, because rather than arguing with the cop, as I might have in the past, I smiled at him, hoping he would see that I was operating on a higher plane. Ommmmmmmmmm.

Unfortunately, he saw only that I was operating at a higher rate of speed than the law allowed. But even as he wrote out the speeding ticket, he assured me that I could attend traffic school, and thus wipe the whole unpleasant experience off my record. No one really wants to spend eight hours in traffic school, but no one really wants higher insurance rates, either. And so thousands of Californians can be found, on any given weekend, attending the traffic school of their choice.

And boy, do they have choices: singles traffic school, gourmet cooking traffic school, comedy traffic school, to name just a few.

Now, if you're from New York, or from almost anyplace else for that matter, you probably think I'm making this up. In no-nonsense New York, a speeding ticket means dreaded "points." Get enough "points" and you lose your license. No one gives you a shot at redemption, and if they did, they certainly would not want you to enjoy the experience. But in California, redemption and recreation are not mutually exclusive. Aside from the hefty fee for both the ticket and the school, I would have to say it was the most fun I'd had in a punishment mode since one of my high school teachers gave me detention with a leather-jacketed lothario named Neil.

For my traffic school experience, I chose comedy. Not that this was without risk, because, let's face it, being forced to listen to bad jokes for eight hours could be a living hell. I lucked out, however, and got a professional comedian who knew how to keep his audience captive, even though, of course, we already were. We sat in a room painted with clouds and cartoons and we shared our violations, as in, "My name is Judy and I speed." We also shared our *vocations* because no one in L.A. wants to pass up the opportunity for a little "networking," which is L.A.-speak for hitting on someone and maybe, just maybe, getting lucky. In this class, there was a private eye who specialized in protecting actresses, a casting director for *Dr. Quinn, Medicine Woman,* and a psychologist from Malibu who confessed she had trouble obeying the speed limit. "What's the matter," the instructor asked her, "some unresolved issues?"

She probably felt better after we all had engaged in a bit of psychodrama, in which we wadded up pieces of paper and threw them at people in the room who reminded us of cops. I know I felt better, and feeling better is what really counts in California.

As for driving better, that's an open question. About a year and a half later, I was once again pulled over, this time for passing on the right shoulder. Normally, I would never do such a thing, but I was late to my appointment with my therapist.

"So," said the motorcycle cop who leaned into my window, "would you like a ticket for passing on the right or for not wearing a seat belt?"

Can you imagine a New York cop making such an offer?

"Um, the seat belt? I'm sorry, officer, but I was rushing to my therapy appointment."

"I'll tell you what," he said, "why don't you call her while I'm writing the ticket and explain why you're running late." And he nodded toward my car phone.

As I was telling my therapist the details of my delay, the cop once again leaned into the car and shouted at the phone: *"Tell her to slow down!"*

It just doesn't get any more California than that.

After a while, my kids and I started collecting L.A. moments, the sorts of moments we never, ever would have experienced in Metuchen, New Jersey. Like coming around a corner at the supermarket and crashing our grocery cart into Dom DeLuise's grocery cart and hearing him say, in a perfect parody of a car accident, his hands raised in mock horror: "Let's just thank *God* no one was hurt. That's the important thing!"

Like the day I knew my daughter was over the thrill of sighting Hollywood stars, when she came back from jogging and announced, furiously, "That Roseanne Barr almost ran me down! She wasn't even *looking!*"

Or like the time I ran into a homeless man on my way out of a Subway, after I'd purchased a deli sandwich special.

"Can you spare a buck?" he asked.

"I'm sorry. Honestly, I just spent my last dollar on this lunch."

He looked down at his feet.

"But I'll tell you what," I added, "you can have this bag of potato chips that came with my order."

He gave me a withering look and said, with more than a twinge of contempt, "Thanks, but no thanks. Those things are full of fat, you know."

I wouldn't be surprised if he had a personal trainer, as well. Everyone else does. And I have *no* doubt that he was writing a screenplay. He might even have had a publicist.

Publicists sprout like palm trees in Los Angeles. They are so ubiquitous that it's hard to practice journalism without bumping into them. I was doing a story on Road Rage, and my producer, Carmen Dixon, had arranged for us to go on a "drive-along" with a man suffering from this particular malady and his therapist, who specialized in treating it. (I'm tempted to say "only in L.A." at this point, but how many times can you say it?) We got into an enormous Chevy Suburban, the "rager" at the wheel, the therapist directly behind him, and my cameraman, Skip Jennings, in the front passenger seat so he could record all the action. Carmen and I, along with sound man Mel Barr, sat in the rear.

As we drove along, and the predictable L.A. traffic horrors began to eat away at our subject's composure, the therapist encouraged him to "share his feelings in the moment," the moment being our subject screaming *"shithead"* at another driver while leaning on the horn. After "talking him down," the therapist turned to me to answer questions about his therapeutic methods. After going on at some length, I heard another voice pipe up.

"Keep your answers short. Soundbites are usually no more than fifteen seconds."

My producer and I turned around to see where this voice was coming from, and spotted a man sitting in the stern of this enormous boat of a car. He smiled.

This man was, it turns out, the therapist's publicist.

As I started to protest his interruptions, he pre-empted me with, "I just *have* to tell you, I'm *such* a fan."

"Fan?"

"Why, yes! Of your work!"

Yet another moment of recognition undermined by reality.

"Thank you very much, but it really isn't helpful to have someone coaching the doctor while we interview him."

The driver was screaming, *"Asshole!"*

I suddenly knew just how he felt.

Ironically, Californians only seem tense while driving. The rest of the time, they are pretty laid back. This might be a response to the ever-present threat of very real disasters—brush fires, earthquakes, mudslides, riots, the Oscars—a sort of don't-sweat-the-small-stuff attitude that masks an underlying terror that the big stuff may be just around the corner.

When I first arrived in L.A., the CBS bureau chief, Jennifer Siebens, invited me over to her house for a party. She lived high in the Hollywood Hills, and we sat out on her patio looking at the lights of L.A. twinkling in the valley below. We also looked at the bright-red flames of a brush fire in the hills above. As those flames licked their way up the hill, I began to get nervous. Here

I was, a new correspondent for ABC, and I was looking right at what I thought surely would be a *story.*

And yet, none of the CBS correspondents sitting around me seemed the slightest bit concerned.

I turned to David Dow and said, "I wonder if I should call my bureau?"

"Nah," he said, leaning back in his chair, "that's not a network fire."

"How can you tell?"

"It's not a network fire until it crawls up that hill, down the other side, and up the next hill. And it will have to destroy at least six multi-million-dollar estates along the way. And maybe not even then."

A disaster, in California terms, has to be *very, very big.* And so it was, at 4:31 A.M. on January 17, 1994, when I was awakened by the sound of a freight train rumbling through my condo. I'd love to use a more original metaphor, but sometimes the reason things are cliches is because they are so very apt. So a freight train it is.

I hung on to my bed in my top floor apartment as restless tectonic plates far below me tried to get comfortable after too many years in the same position, thrusting up and out and sending shock waves from the San Fernando Valley east through Hollywood and west through coastal communities like mine. As my bed turned into a trampoline, I heard furniture toppling all over the apartment, the sounds of crashing glass, of water actually *sloshing out of the toilets* and underneath it all, this terrible, terrifying rumbling sound. I looked up and saw the top of my wall separate from the ceiling. I looked out my window, which usually frames a heavenly view of the ocean, to see the hellish sight of electrical transformers blowing all the way down the coast, entire communities going dark.

It occurred to me, as I'm sure it did to thousands of other Angelenos, that I might die. At least, I thought, I'm on the top floor, so when they start digging, I'll be among the first to be pulled from the rubble. You'd be amazed at the selfish thoughts that spring to mind at a moment like that.

It also would have been a *swell* moment to have someone at my side, someone to hold on to. The kids were in school at U.C. Berkeley (which is smack dab on the Hayward Fault, something I began to obsess about after this experience) and the closest human beings were the married couple across the hall and, a few doors down, a transsexual named Linda. At that moment, even Linda would have looked good to me (as she did, actually, when she came into the dark hallway later, dressed in an elegant peignoir, asking in a sleepy baritone: "Is everyone all right?").

When the rumbling stopped, I stepped gingerly onto the floor, now strewn with personal detritus, basically everything I owned. I made a mental note to put flipflops under the bed from now on, as I tiptoed through broken glass and mirrors stretching into the hallway. There, I found the breakfront on its belly, the cabinet doors ripped off in the impact, my grandmother's bone china teacups mere shards of their former selves. The fatally wounded furniture was jammed up against the front door, blocking my exit. Just then, I heard the phone ring.

I stumbled toward the kitchen, and dug out the phone from underneath what seemed to be a ton of debris—books from the shelves and food from the cabinets.

"Hello?" I said, surprised by the tremulant sound of my own voice, easily a 5.5 on the Richter Scale, I thought. The tremor that prompted it would turn out to be a 6.8.

"Judy? This is the New York desk."

"Yes?"

"There's been an earthquake out there."

This would have been a delicious time to say something off-hand and ironic. But my reaction was pretty much void of either. *"No shit!"*

"We need you to get to your bureau ASAP. They have no phone service there, so we're calling instead."

"Sure," I said. "I had *planned* to get there ASAP." Journalists love using military jargon in times of crisis. "Just as soon as I can find my computer, something to wear, and two earrings that match." Clearly, all that accessory training was not wasted.

After I got dressed, I could hear my neighbors outside in the hall, and I called to them for some help. I managed to lift part of the breakfront, while they opened the door and pushed from the other side. We all descended down the eight flights of stairs together in the dark, our shaky flashlights illuminating large cracks in the walls. We wondered what we would find once we got down to the parking garage.

We were among the lucky ones that night. Our building suffered cosmetic damage, but the main structure was secure. So was my car. As I drove off, all the neighbors who were huddling outside in the parking lot looked at me like I was crazy. *"Gotta go to work!"* I said, having already switched into crazed commuter mode. As I made my way down Pacific Coast Highway, I had to dodge huge boulders and, at one point, a good portion of a house that had slid onto the road, along with most of the hill it once perched on. By the time I got to the "10" freeway, I figured I was home free. Surely, I thought, I must have just seen the worst of the damage.

That's when I saw the cop. All alone, standing in the middle of the freeway, waving frantically in my direction. He was pointing to the exit ramp. I was annoyed, thinking of how much time I would lose by trying to get to work on surface streets, especially with all the traffic lights out. And then, as I exited, I saw why he had looked so frantic. Just ahead, the freeway had collapsed. If he had not been there, I would surely have pulled an Evel Knievel, with nowhere near the same odds of a safe landing.

I picked up my cell phone and called New York. They connected me through to *Good Morning America* and Morton Dean, who was anchoring that day. As I drove through the dark streets of L.A., I described, on air, what I was seeing even as I kept one eye out for falling bricks and debris in the road. As I drove through the poorest part of Hollywood, I saw residents wrapped in blankets, shivering from fear, most of them immigrants from Mexico, where they had learned that going back inside a building after an earthquake is never a good idea. Not that they had much choice *here;* many of the buildings, especially the old brick ones, were in a state of near-collapse. It was not until hours later that news helicopters could get in the air and show us how widespread the devastation was, to show us buildings that *had,* in fact, collapsed, killing the occupants. The image that really stuck with me that morning was the sight of flames emerging from flooded streets, fueled by ruptured gas lines, the ultimate symbol, somehow, for the paradox that is California. Fire and Water, Peril and Paradise, Rubble and Rollerblades, one-stop shopping.

At the bureau, the place was running on generator power, our combination newsroom-studio awash in an eerie light (albeit a rather *flattering* light, which is what really matters). A lot of people had brought their families with them, even their pets. No one wanted to be alone at a time like that. I was directed to the anchor chair. By that time, Ted Koppel was anchoring from the East Coast. The two of us winged it for the next few hours, airing raw video pretty much as it came in, ad-libbing (thank God for that radio training) our way through each reported development. Now *this,* now *that*. And now and *then,* a fumble. When Ted unexpectedly asked me to explain how the Richter Scale works, for example, or when I blurted out a remark that would, to my horror, be among the quotes-of-the-day in the next day's papers.

It came when Ted asked me why I would *choose* to live in L.A., right in the heart of earthquake country.

"First of all," I said, my mouth once again outpacing my brain, "I was assigned to this bureau and I didn't have much choice!"

Fortunately, he laughed. Later, during a commercial break, the electricity suddenly came back on in the studio, switching on every floodlight on the set. I looked in the monitor and saw my overexposed features, white as a ghost and, yes, *angular,* and cried, "Oh *no!*" Although the audience couldn't hear this, Ted could, and so when we went back on the air, he said "I just heard Judy Muller say 'Oh *no.*' Let's rejoin her in L.A. to see if they've had another tremor."

"Oh! *No!*"

Now, I couldn't seem to *stop* saying it.

"Actually, Ted, I was just reacting to all the lights coming back on."

"Well," he chided, "let's watch those 'oh no's,' shall we?"

"Right."

It would be a very long day, the first in a very long week. By the time I got home that night, after reporting for *World News Tonight* and *Nightline* and preparing a piece for the next morning's *GMA* broadcast, I had almost forgotten about the shock of that morning's near-death experience. Until, that is, I opened my front door.

The electricity had come back on, and I could see the wreckage much more clearly. My stereo had flown across the living room, and was in pieces. Every dish and glass in the kitchen cupboards, or what was left of them, covered the floor in a three-inch-deep quagmire that included broken food jars from the refrigerator and shattered wine bottles from the upper cabinets, which is where I stored them for the occasional guest who was *not* an alcoholic. I think it was the stench of the wine that hit me the hardest, which is no surprise, given my particular problem, coupled with the rather compelling thought that a glass of wine would have tasted damn good at that moment. Fortunately, those moments are extremely rare and, in this case, impossible to fulfill, since every drop of liquor was now mixed with bits of glass.

So I did what any other tough trekker who'd survived her share of cougar attacks would do. I sat down and cried.

Then I cleared a path from the front door to the bathroom to my bed. That was all the cleaning up I would get around to for at least a week. I also let a news crew come over to shoot b-roll, which ended up in their file of generic earthquake shots. Never did I dream that the video would pop up the next Sunday on *This Week with David Brinkley.*

I had just finished a live shot, chatting with David as I stood in front of the collapsed freeway that had almost claimed my car earlier in the week, when he surprised me by saying, "You've been indefatigable this week, Judy."

I just had time to take in the compliment and marvel that he would risk the word "indefatigable" during a live shot, when he added, "and I understand you suffered a lot of damage at your place, too."

"Well, not really . . ." I was thinking of other friends at the bureau who'd had to move out after their homes slid right off the foundations. Not to mention the people who had *died*.

"We have some videotape of that damage," he said. "We're showing that right now." (They were *what?*) "Thank you for the good work while you've been going through all that."

Talk about embarrassing. I never dreamed that the b-roll of my place would be showcased in such a way. And it didn't end there. Everywhere I went, for months afterward, people would say, "Hey, aren't you the reporter who suffered all the damage in the earthquake?" This even happened to me while I was on vacation in New Zealand where, I learned, this particular clip had aired.

Recognized, yet again, for the wrong reasons.

As I say, I was among the lucky ones. I had earthquake insurance and most of the damage was covered. But the emotional trauma is something we all share. It's never far from the surface; all it takes is someone bumping your desk, and you're ready to hit the floor. Every minor tremor, no matter how short-lived, ratchets up the adrenalin one more time, providing one more reminder of how powerless we are. That may sound trite on a sunny day at the beach, but it tends to be downright profound in the dark, holding on to your bed for dear life, as your belongings crash down around you.

In other words, context is everything. And that's true not just of those personally memorable moments, but the professional ones, as well. Getting a little time and distance does wonders for one's perspective.

Which is one reason why it's nice to re-visit a story after a certain amount of time. Years after a group of LAPD officers beat up Rodney King with batons, tasers, and kicks, caught on video for all the horrified world to see, I did a *Nightline* piece to see what had happened to all the characters in that event, one that had incited riots, property damage, and even death, not to mention a major investigation into the way the police do business (and, as it turned out, not for the last time).

The two most interesting interviews were with Tim Wind, the only rookie officer out there that night, and Rodney King himself. Wind had been acquitted of criminal charges, not only in the Simi Valley trial but in the federal trial, as well. He had been found not liable for King's injuries by a civil jury. And a police inquiry cleared him, as well. Nevertheless, he had been fired from the LAPD and had had a terrible time finding work. He had to have surgery for intestinal problems brought on by stress and he was still shunned wherever he went. His life, he told us, was hell.

Not so Rodney King. As you may recall, he had been drunk the night he led police on a high-speed chase, fearful of being taken in for violating parole. He'd taken a pretty bad beating and, because it had been caught on videotape, got a pretty good settlement. When I interviewed King, he was anticipating the debut of his rap record label, financed in part with that settlement. The interview took place at the office of his lawyer, who sat very close by, along with a couple of nervous-looking folks, including, perhaps, a publicist.

I'd always wondered how much pain and suffering could have been avoided, both for him and the city, if King had gotten sober before any of this had happened. Even after the beating incident (which would certainly qualify as "a bottom" where I come from), he continued to be picked up for various infractions, almost always linked to alcohol abuse. So I asked him how he was doing with his drinking problem.

"I don't do things like that anymore," he said, somewhat ambiguously. He seemed reluctant to elaborate, much less actually admit he even had a problem, so I pushed on to other subjects. After we'd covered most of the key points, I said, "Just one last question."

At hearing that, you could see him visibly relaxing, almost exhaling with relief, a sigh echoed by the line-up of lawyers.

"Just one last question" is a very effective device.

"Do you sometimes wish it had never happened at all?"

He smiled broadly, and said, "Are you kidding? I wouldn't have all *this!*" He motioned to his soon-to-be-released CD.

And then he winked.

It was astonishing. If he had said anything like that at the *time,* it would have been downright provocative. One of his lawyers cornered me as we started to break down our equipment.

"You're not going to use that last bit, are you? He was just kidding."

"Kidding or not, he said it to our camera and he knew it was part of the interview."

All the way out the door, they kept on pleading. The piece aired with the quote intact. Lou Cannon, author of a book about the Rodney King case, called and asked if any other media had picked up on that quote. "That's *news*," he said. Actually, the only person who *did* pick up on it was Anna Deveare Smith, the author and actress who had written a one-woman play about the case. She said she was updating the script and wanted to include that provocative moment.

Otherwise, no one seemed terribly interested. I suppose it's more comfortable to be left with our initial black-and-white impressions. Gray just confuses things. I imagine Rodney King will always be remembered for one quote, and one quote only: "Can't we all just get along?"

Besides, Rodney King was history long before the *Nightline* "where are they now" story ever aired. In spite of the enormous impact of the King case, from the devastation of South Central L.A. (which has never really recovered) to the inflaming of racial tensions, it couldn't hold a candle to the spectacle of O. J. Simpson, a case which would end up consuming almost two years of my life.

CHAPTER

10

OD'ING ON
O. J.

No me recuerdo, señor.

—ROSA LOPEZ

I f you, like Rosa, can't remember the details, consider yourself fortunate. I can't *forget* the details, which is not surpris-
ing, since I was riveted to the courtroom proceedings,
criminal and civil, for a very long time.

Rosa Lopez, for those who might have forgotten, was the
housekeeper who worked at the home next door to O. J. Simpson. She was my favorite witness. The plucky lady from El Salvador wanted absolutely nothing to do with the trial of the
century and, in so many words, told Judge Ito so. At one point,
as Ito tried to cajole her into cooperating, Senora Lopez said,
"No. I'm tired."

And she turned on her heel and walked straight out the
courtroom door, past the Goldmans, the press corps, all the visiting celebrities (getting a seat at the trial had become a *must* for
everyone who was *anyone*). Rosa, to her credit, *did not give a
damn!*

Not so the rest of the country. At one point, a poll told us that
something like 45 percent of all Americans were keeping up
with the case, and a hardcore 13 percent were tuning in *daily.*

Thirteen percent of the population is a lot of people, people who were, let's face it, obsessed. Many of those people lived here. Many of them, in fact, were (and still are) my friends. No sooner had Simpson been accused (which, for those of us who knew nothing about his record of spousal abuse, was akin to calling Donald Duck a serial killer), than theories started flying. Keep in mind that I live in a community of screenwriters, all searching for a good story. And here it was, right in our own neighborhood.

I used to drive down Bundy (where Nicole's condo was located) almost every day. After the murders, I almost never drove down Bundy; the traffic jams made it impossible. I also used to run into Simpson at the local dry cleaners. When I mentioned this to a reporter from Virginia who was doing a story on the press covering the trial, it ended up in his article as "Judy Muller often ran into O. J. Simpson at a laundromat in Brentwood." I wonder if there are some Virginians out there who have an image of me and O. J., side by side, folding our unmentionables. I hope not.

At any rate, from the get-go, my writer friends started calling me with what they believed were "good leads," leads which left no suspect unturned, from the Akita to the Mafia. My friends Kathy and Alan, a married screenwriting couple, became so absorbed they took to driving around the neighborhood, clocking the times it would have taken for Simpson to take various routes and speculating on various places he might have stopped along the way. Another friend, David Lifton, an author who has written extensively about the Kennedy assassination, also weighed in, via fax. In no fewer than nine pages, with footnotes and subheadings like "The Missing Time Period," he suggested checking out such places as "Public Toilet #12" in a local park as a possible location where the suspect might have cleaned up and changed his clothes.

I couldn't really blame them for their obsession. All of them were facing deadlines on various writing projects. As any writer can tell you, almost any distraction, from repeated trips to the refrigerator to watching reruns of *Gilligan's Island,* beats sitting down at the computer and actually *writing.* For example, I have gained five pounds on this chapter alone.

So give them a case like O. J. Simpson and they will run with it. Kathy and Alan were especially proud of the moment when their amateur detective skills unmasked the profession of a key witness, Pablo Fenvjes. You don't remember Pablo? He was Nicole's neighbor who told the court that he heard the "plaintive wail" of a dog right about the time of the murders. Kathy and Alan immediately suspected *(aha!)* that the only person who would use such a phrase would be a screenwriter. Anyone else would have said "bark" or "howl." Sure enough, they found Pablo's name in the Writer's Guild Directory.

Who cares? Well, no one. No one except the hardcore trial-followers, like another one of my friends, Terry Louise Fisher, a former prosecutor and co-creator and writer of the TV series *L.A. Law.* Like so many writers, Terry works at home. Once O. J. hit the TV screen, the computer screen didn't have a chance. I'd be sitting in our *Nightline* office, watching the trial on a bank of monitors (now and then, I'd go to court, but for our purposes, the view from the camera's eye was the only one that counted) and taking notes on my computer, when Terry would call.

"What's she *doing?*"

"Who?"

"Marcia Clark! It's driving me *crazy!*"

And she would go on to explain how it *should* be done, an explanation that always made enormous sense to me and made me wish I could direct her call straight through to the courtroom, just to even the playing field a bit. Whenever Terry and I and the other O. J.-philes get together now, so many years after the case ended, we still amuse ourselves with pathetic little memory games. "All right, who said to the jurors, 'You have to save Baby Justice?' " (Chris Darden). "And what master of sarcasm said, 'Is *that it,* Mr. Fung?' " (Barry Scheck).

I must admit I have something of an advantage on this score. Our *Nightline* office was papered in quotes, memorably absurd phrases we would write down each day and post on the walls, like so much graffiti in a prison cell (an apt metaphor, actually, since the trial took a cruel and unusual amount of time).

Some of these quotes of the day were gleaned from the medical experts:

> "The person got cut during the dynamic process of the altercation";
>
> "The four F's of adrenalin are fear, flight, fight, and, um, mating";
>
> "Compare and contrast DQ-Alpha and D-1S80" (the jury, as you can imagine, was spellbound by this DNA stuff, which lasted through all of April, truly the cruelest month);
>
> "Contaminated, compromised, corrupted" (easy to remember if sung to the tune of "Bewitched, Bothered, and Bewildered").

Police testimony also provided some notable quotables, as in, "We were flagged down by two witnesses and a dog."

Ditto, the legalese of lawyers: "At some time, did that recital end?"

Rarely did a day go by when we couldn't find a suitable quote for our walls. In fact, I can remember only one such day, when we were desperate enough to allow in *any* quote coming from the bank of television monitors. That day's winner was from a soap opera character who said, "I can't service cars all day and you all night." Who says there's no art in daytime TV?

But for the most part, the trial was a rich source for mangled English. "Let's calendar that," Judge Ito would say on a regular basis, prompting a wince from anyone who still cares about the difference between a noun and verb. On the other hand, the trial also introduced a lot of new phrases into the national vocabulary. We learned, for example, that one exception to the no-hearsay-allowed rule in testimony is "the excited utterance." That in-cludes something a person says during a moment of duress, the theory being that most people don't lie at those moments.

In the Simpson case, for example, Nicole may have been making an "excited utterance"—albeit a long one—when she was on the phone with a 911 operator while O. J. was breaking down the back door.

Here in L.A., land of earthquake, flood, and fire, the excited utterance is not an uncommon thing. And now, at last, we had a name for it! During the trial, I overheard O. J.-watchers arguing at a party and one of them uttered, excitedly, "It does *too* qualify as an excited utterance. If that's not an excited utterance, I don't know what is!"

For a former English teacher like myself, the real treat was the rare occasion when the language was used skillfully. F. Lee Bailey, cross-examining a psychologist on the subject of spousal abuse, said, "Do you and others of your—ilk—all subscribe to this theory?"

When it comes to the implied insult, you can't do much better than "ilk," especially when preceded by a pregnant pause and delivered in a sac of sarcasm.

Likewise, you never heard the defense use the phrases "domestic violence" or "spousal abuse." They used the phrase "marital discord," a much gentler spin on the subject. And when it came to the language of racism, a subject raised during the testimony of Detective Mark Fuhrman, the defense team again used the power of suggestion. An entire day was spent on this subject, as the black prosecutor, Chris Darden, argued that a racist term uttered by Fuhrman should never be allowed in testimony because it would prejudice the jurors, most of whom were black. The black defense attorney, Johnnie Cochran, countered that to imply that the black jurors could not rise above the power of what he called the "N-word" and render an impartial verdict was an insult to African Americans everywhere.

Throughout this debate, no one actually *used* the N-word. The defense team clearly understood the power of understatement. Had they repeatedly used the N-word before the climactic confrontation with Fuhrman, it would have been significantly drained of its power, much ado about N.

Throughout the trial, I would be bombarded with questions from well-meaning friends, questions along the lines of, "So tell us, what's really going on? What do you know that you haven't told us?" I always find this fascinating, this suspicion that reporters are privy to the *real* story which, for some reason, we just don't want to share with the outside world. Fact is, we get our inside information the old-fashioned way, by stumbling over it. Which wasn't hard to do in this case, especially in a town where everyone seemed to be either a sleuth, a source, or a suspect. One week, when I was getting a quick haircut at my usual place, which just happened to be a few blocks from the murder scene, I asked my hairdresser how she'd been and she said, with a sigh, "Well, I just wish these reporters would quit hounding me."

"Why would reporters be hounding you?"

"Oh, I guess because I was such a good friend of Nicole's."

"You *were?*"

"Yeah. We used to model together and I used to double-date with her and O. J."

Being the sensitive soul that I am, I immediately began to hound her, as well, firing one question after another, as she snipped away at my hair. And yes, I did learn something very valuable from this encounter. I learned that you should never distract your hairdresser unless you're willing to emerge with a head looking very much like a coconut.

For all its diversions, from mangled language to mangled haircuts, the Simpson case always had an overriding significance that gave it real gravity. It mattered for what it told us about our justice system, the different ways that system was perceived and the different ways that system could be manipulated. And for the families of the victims, of course, it mattered for reasons that no one can understand who hasn't been through a similar loss. Only one reporter I know of who covered the trial, Dominick Dunne, could make such a claim; some years before, his own daughter had been murdered. Perhaps that's why, on the day the verdict came in, I was immediately drawn to the look on Dunne's face as he sat in the courtroom. He had a stunned expression, one that gave new meaning to "jaw-dropping." For millions of Americans, whose jaws dropped at the same time, it was an unforgettable moment.

But at our *Nightline* studio, we didn't have much time to ponder that moment. We raced to put on an hour-long show about the verdict and the country's reaction to it. And because of the power of those reverberations, we did the same thing for at least five nights running. If I had known, going into that week, how much copy I would be expected to produce, I doubt that I could've faced it. Fortunately, in the news business, you never know what you're going to have to face until you're *up* to your face in the reality of it. Never-ending now this-ness.

By the time the civil trial rolled around, then, no wonder folks were sick of it all. And yet, in many ways, that second trial was much more fascinating than the first. For one thing, O. J. Simpson was free to mingle with reporters, which presented a number of uncomfortable moments. I remember going through the magnetometer right after Simpson, and the security guard finding a pocket knife I often carry in my purse. It happened to be a Swiss Army knife, like the ones Simpson reportedly owned. He has also been a pitchman for the company.

As the guard drew the knife out of my purse, O. J. turned and said, with a grin, "Tch, tch, you should know better!"

It was creepy.

This was also the trial in which Simpson finally took the stand, since criminal penalties were no longer an issue. We got to see a true narcissist in action, one who could pathologically cling to his story no matter how compelling the evidence against him.

"I never hit Nicole," he'd say, at the same time adding, "but I take responsibility for that," "that" being a blown-up picture of Nicole's battered face, on display in front of the jury. He also denied that the rare Bruno Magli shoes worn by the murderer were his, even though more than thirty photos by various photographers placed his feet squarely in those "ugly-assed shoes," as he put it. You had to at least give him points for the consistency of his inconsistency. This jury, however, gave him *no* points for veracity.

The civil trial, at the Santa Monica courthouse, did not allow in cameras, which was too bad, really, because the same country that had been split over the first verdict might have benefitted from seeing Simpson on the stand. Since I could no longer view the trial on a TV monitor, I tried to be in the courtroom every day, which provided an interesting view of the back of Simpson's head and an earful of ironic remarks from my seatmates, satirist Harry Shearer and commentator Star Jones.

On the days when it was too crowded in the courtroom for both Cynthia McFadden (who was covering it for *World News Tonight*) and myself, I would head for the audio trailer, located in the parking lot across the street from the courthouse, an area referred to irreverently as Camp O. J.-Sur-La-Mer. One of my colleagues likened the group gathered in the audio trailer to the bar scene from *Star Wars*. And certainly it was quite a collection: some of the world's most famous legal eagles, "the commentatorati," as Harry Shearer called them, all perched on metal chairs, all facing front, in the direction of two huge speakers. On one particularly momentous day, when Simpson first took the stand, the crowd included Defense Attorney Leslie Abramson of

Menendez fame; former District Attorney Ira Reiner; feminist attorney Gloria Allred (one memorable protest sign outside the courthouse read: "Caution! Do *not* get between Gloria Allred and a camera!"); former Judge Burton Katz; bestselling authors Jeff Toobin and Larry Schiller; a handful of law professors-turned-pundits, including Peter Arenella and Laurie Levenson; and former Simpson defense attorney Robert Shapiro, who actually believed for a while that he could be a commentator without violating attorney-client privilege.

Also present, of course, were the journalists, including this one, who had made them what they are by demanding pithy soundbites at the drop of a glove. We had, in fact, created a new made-for-TV species: pundits in pancake, equipped with earpieces connected to IFB cords curling down their backs, ready to be plugged in to the nearest camera.

With the commentatorati all in place, it was hard for any one to really stand out, but on this day, as everyone waited for testimony to begin, the door to the audio trailer suddenly swung open. The room went silent. There, backlit by the western sun, stood a tall, buckskin-fringed silhouette. It was as though the saloon door had just swung open to reveal none other than Billy the Kid. Only this was Gerry the Spence, who could be just as intimidating, a wordslinger from out of town, hired by the show called *Extra* to spin his stuff.

Yes, quite an impressive gathering. And even though the Simpson case had to come to an end eventually, some of these folks would migrate to other trials, other stories, not to mention to their own television shows and book deals. The Simpson circus had become, in fact, a booming business, one that still logged a lot of miles long after the tents had folded in L.A.

Five years later, proof of the case's staying power came crawling through the fax machine in our bureau. It was immediately handed to me, as the only person there who still gave a damn. Now, our newsroom gets a lot of press releases every week, most of them forgettable. This one was not only unforgettable, but almost unbelievable. On the stationery of a public relations firm, it read, "Ron Shipp, former LAPD officer in the Nicole Brown Simpson murder, has spent many years grieving Nicole's death and reflecting on his testimony. Now healed, five years after her death, Ron, a *key witness* in that very publicized case, is dedicating his life to speaking out against domestic violence."

Now, I suppose there *were* people out there who had been asking, "I wonder what ever happened to that key witness in the O. J. Simpson trial, Ron Shipp? I wonder if he's gotten past his grief. Will he *ever* stop reflecting on his testimony and get on with his life?"

At last, we had the answer. This was the most stunning revelation since we had learned that O. J.'s pal A. C. Cowlings had landed a job as a sales rep for, of all things, a *shoe* company. O. J. himself, of course, was still taking time out from his search for the real killers to date women who bore a creepy resemblance to the late Nicole. Rosa Lopez was said to have returned to El Salvador where, rumor had it, she married a ventriloquist. She may be the only one who never got a publicist. But, thank God, Ron Shipp is available for motivational speeches. Just have your people call his people.

The trial was a turning point for "my" people as well.

In the last days of the civil trial, before the verdict was delivered smack dab in the middle of the President's televised State of the Union Address (talk about your ethical dilemmas!), I spotted a new journalist wandering around Camp O. J.-Sur-La-Mer. She was looking for the CBS trailer. I recognized her, of course, because she was (and still is) my daughter. But she was dressed like an adult, which threw me for a moment, and even appeared to be acting like one. It was the first time we had shown up at the same story at the same time. But it wouldn't be the last.

CHAPTER

11

———

THE
SERPENT'S
TOOTH

———

How sharper than a serpent's tooth it is
to have a thankless child.

— S H A K E S P E A R E

Of course, Lear was not entirely on the mark with the "thankless child" thing. At least Cordelia turned out to be a truly loving daughter. She simply made the mistake of replying with humor at a moment when her father lost his. Even so, is there anything more frightening than having your child reflect back your own finely honed sense of irony? Actually, there is. It's when they beat you at your own game.

I suppose I have no one but myself to blame for the fact that I now have a daughter working in the same field. While my younger daughter, Kerry, has the heart and soul of an artist, my older daughter, Kristen, has the killer instincts of a journalist. As in: "She'd walk over her own mother for a good story," a phrase not usually meant in the literal sense.

But as I said, I alone bear the responsibility. This is a kid, after all, whose baby book was filled, not with her first words, but with her first headlines. "No one else I know," she once complained, "has a baby book with a clipping that reads, *'Nixon resigns.'* "

As I mentioned earlier, even as my kids were immersed in current event material, they often found themselves *used* as material. First in my radio commentaries at CBS, then in various magazine articles, and finally, in occasional guest appearances in my Internet column and on NPR. What better way, after all, to humanize an issue than to quote your own kids, whether the subject is education or teenage drinking? And what better way to humiliate them in front of their friends?

"Okay, Mom," Kristen would fume after she'd been quoted back to herself at school, *"enough!* Isn't anything off the *record* around here?"

"Of course, honey," I'd reply, even as I swelled with pride that she had picked up the concept of "off the record."

The only time they seemed even remotely proud of my writing was when I was published in *Sports Illustrated*. The same fly-fishing article that had prompted the long-awaited pardon from Dan Rather also impressed some of the cooler boys in their school, prompting a few to stop by for an autograph and providing a vivid lesson in how to reel 'em in with a good story.

They also learned to keep abreast of the news in a way that eluded most teenagers. I'd like to say their interest was sparked by our scintillating dinnertime discussions. But that would be a lie. They kept up with current events as a way of predicting when I might be on the road.

I rarely traveled when I was with CBS Radio, but once my kids were teenagers, I did accept the occasional assignment out of town for a few days, thinking (or not thinking, as it turned out), that they were responsible young women. But then, I could remember just how "responsible" I had been at that age (the curse of all parents who were adolescents in the sixties), so to make *sure,* I asked them to sign a pledge *on their word of honor* that they would not allow any friends in the house while I was gone. It's quite possible that the phrase "upon penalty of death" may have been in there somewhere. Whatever the threat, implied or otherwise, the underlying concept was *honor,* a concept I actually thought meant something in our house.

If you detect an unresolved resentment, you'd be right. Let this be a warning to parents everywhere: When it comes to teenagers, hormones trump honor every time.

I did not learn of their nefarious betrayal until we had moved to California and the yearbook arrived from their old school in New Jersey. Next to each class photo was a category called "Favorite Moment." Almost all of their friends had written: "Muller House, June 14."

"Odd," I thought. "I don't remember anything special about that date." So I looked it up on my old calendar.

It was a Saturday, that "favorite moment" for so many of Metuchen's youth. It was a Saturday when I happened to be in San Francisco covering the International Aids Conference. A Saturday that will live in infamy, at least in our family.

When I confronted the criminals, they confessed almost eagerly, figuring, I suppose, that the statute of limitations had expired by then. What were the chances, they thought, of being grounded for something that happened almost a year ago in another jurisdiction? Out spilled the details of a party that had been planned with near-perfect precision. Kerry told me (a bit too proudly for my taste), how they had moved all the downstairs furniture upstairs, rolled up all the rugs and stowed all breakables. She put pieces of masking tape on tables to show exactly where knick-knacks had been, tape on the floor to show where the furniture had been, so that my perfectionist eye would see nothing amiss later. And I never did, so I guess her calling as a designer/artist is spot-on.

"Was this a one-time offense?" I asked, hopefully.

They looked at each other and grinned, serpents' teeth agleaming.

"Well," said Kristen, "there was the space shuttle. My friends heard you reporting the launch from Cape Canaveral and figured we might as well launch another party. But don't worry, Mom." She paused for effect. "It never really got off the ground."

Despite her complete and utter lack of remorse, I had to admire her delivery. She was well on her way, I thought, to weaseling her way out of a tight situation with a well-turned phrase—no small talent in a writer!

Later, when the girls were at Berkeley, Kristen suddenly announced that she might like to be a reporter. I knew she had signed up for an investigative journalism class taught by *60 Minutes* producer Lowell Bergman, but I hadn't realized her future aspirations were in that direction. She was a political science major and, I figured, headed for some sort of activist role in politics.

I was flattered. "You mean," I said, setting myself up, "that you'd actually like to follow in my footsteps?"

"God, no. I mean a *real* journalist, one who writes for a newspaper. Preferably, an *alternative* newspaper."

I never did find out just what that meant. I assume it had to do with the theory that underground papers were the only honest alternative to a mainstream press that had sold out to corporate interests, a concept I would never *publicly* endorse, lest the little white-gloved hand that feeds me take offense. But, of course, she is my child, and questioning the status quo is probably inbred. So while my ego was somewhat deflated, I still felt a little surge of pride at her anti-establishment stance.

It was not a stance that lasted long, however. Her alternative press plans became moot once she graduated and found out there is no such thing as alternative rent.

That's when Kristen called the CBS bureau in Los Angeles, where she had spent a summer as a news intern, and asked if they had any openings. At first, her job as a desk assistant filled me with maternal pride and protective instincts. She'd call almost daily, whispering such furtive questions as, "What are O-and-O's? And why do we hate them?"

How cute, I thought, as I patiently explained, Momma Bird to Fledgling, that an "O-and-O" is a station owned and operated by the network, and that the relationship is often fraught with rivalry and one-up-manship. Little did I know that we were about to develop an O-and-O relationship of our own.

The first troubling signs came after she was promoted to assignment editor, with responsibilities that included finding good stories in the western region and tracking down interviews for *The Evening News with Dan Rather.* In other words, our competition. Her inventive efforts to try and figure out what stories I was working on (and vice versa) turned our once-honest, soul-sharing, mother-daughter bonding conversations into dialogues that sounded like something from that old *Mad* magazine cartoon, "Spy Versus Spy."

Me: "I have to go out of town for a few days. You can reach me on my pager."

Her (in a casual tone): "So, where are you going?"

Me: "Good try."

But she wasn't through with me yet.

"Just tell me one thing. You're not working on a story I've *missed,* are you, something that will get me in *trouble?"*

Oooooh, she's good, I thought. She could break the Omerta of the Mafia, land an interview with J. D. Salinger, talk O. J. into confessing.

But all I said was, "No, you don't have to worry."

And then, of course, *I'd* worry that she would, indeed, get in trouble for missing something. But I'm proud to say she never broke me. At least, not as of this writing.

I suppose it was inevitable that we would eventually find ourselves covering the same story, trying to beat each other to the scoop. The first serious collision along these lines occurred during the group suicide of the Heaven's Gate cult near San Diego. You may remember the story: All the suicides dressed in gymsuits and Nikes (dubbed by one ghoulish observer as "Cross-Over-Jordans"), taking poison in the hopes of hitching a ride on a spaceship they believed to be following in the wake of the Hale-Bopp Comet. The hitchhikers' bodies were discovered in the evening, after the network news programs were over. That meant scrambling for upcoming shows like *Nightline* and *Good Morning America.* My colleague Brian Rooney took a helicopter to report from the scene, while I lined up interviews from the bureau.

Kristen called about an hour into that effort. I could tell, from the background noise, that she was at the CBS bureau.

"Soooo, watcha workin' on?" she asked. I could almost swear she yawned.

"Probably the same thing you're working on. Why *else* would either of us be at work at this time of night?"

A sudden switch in tone, from nonchalance to neediness: "I'm trying to find some experts on cult behavior. Know any?"

"Why should I do your work for you?" I asked in my best "tough love" voice.

"Because," she said in an appalled tone, "I'm your *daughter!*"

"Well," softening a bit now, "who have you found so far?"

A pause at the other end, a long pause, and then, "Why should I tell *you?*"

"Twenty-five hours of labor," I shot back, "and a C-section scar!"

"No *fair,* Mom!" she retorted, hoping against hope that Murphy Brown would take a short coffee break and that my maternal instincts might still surface. Which they did, just enough to give her a hint. When I told her I was about to go to the home of a psychiatrist from UCLA for an interview, she almost shrieked.

"Dr. *West?* But I've lined him up for *tomorrow!*"

"Too bad," I said. "You gotta move fast in this business."

(An aside from the Serpent's Tooth: She takes issue with my version of these events. I feel it only fair to note that she remembers it as *my* asking *her* for Dr. West's phone number. Ever the adult in this relationship, I can only say, "It's my book. Go write your own.")

At any rate, my advice that "you have to move fast in this business" did not go unheeded. As I drove up to Dr. West's home that night, on a dark street in Westwood, I thought I saw a familiar car parked in the driveway.

"No," I gasped. "It couldn't be. She couldn't be that ruthless."

But sure enough, it was Kristen's old yellow Jeep, the same Jeep that had once carried me back and forth from New Jersey to New York in the wee hours of the morning *for years and years and years* to support the same little upstart that had now driven that *very same vehicle* to this critical intersection in our lives.

Only a parent who is still paying their kid's car insurance can understand the depth of this betrayal.

Kristen was standing on the front porch, waiting impatiently for her camera crew to arrive. I quickly joined her there, and we were soon arguing.

"How *could* you?" I asked her.

"You'd do the same thing if you were in my shoes," she said.

She had me there. As I stood on that porch, sputtering and trying to think of a logical rejoinder, the door opened. Dr. West, who knew me from a previous interview, took in the strange drama unfolding on his front stoop and brought the full powers of his psychoanalytic skills to the situation. He also noted the obvious, which is that from our blonde hair to our blue eyes to the stubborn set of our jaws, we were clearly a matched set, the Tweedledee and Tweedledum of Tenacity.

You could almost hear the gears turning in his head, as he strained to remember the names of the two people who had called for an interview, one from ABC, one from CBS.

"*Ohhhh!*" he said with delight, "Muller and Muller! I get it. Wow. What a fascinating dynamic! I'd *love* to study this one."

As it turned out, I got the interview first because her crew was late. But she managed to get the last laugh. Kristen called me at home later and said, "Oh, by the way."

Uh-oh, I thought. "By the way" is never good, not in a family where ironic understatement is an art.

"Mrs. West came up to me before I left, looking kind of embarrassed, and said, 'I think this belongs to your mother.' "

"What belongs to your mother?"

"She handed me this really gross fake nail. Talk about embarrassing!"

Apparently, I'd knocked off a false nail tip that had been applied to mend a broken nail. And I could tell that she wasn't the *slightest* bit embarrassed to deliver the news of its recovery. In fact, she was downright delighted.

Well, as Dr. West said, "It's a fascinating dynamic." And it continues to be, even though Kristen has left my immediate arena and gone on to a job as an associate producer at *60 Minutes II*. Where once my pride was tempered by my paranoia that she would beat me to the punch, now I found my pride being nibbled away by sheer envy. If there is one broadcast that has always been considered the pinnacle to a career in broadcasting, it's *60 Minutes*. And here she was, *starting out* there at the age of twenty-five. And, to set the record straight, she did it without my help, even though I know the perception of influence worried her.

Which is why she was so relieved when the executive producer popped his head in her office one day and said, "Are you Judy Muller's daughter?"

"Yes," said Kristen in surprise.

"Imagine that," he said, shaking his head and walking on down the hall. "Judy Muller's daughter."

When she called to relate this to me, I at first failed to see the point.

"Don't you *see?* That's the man who *hired* me! And he didn't know who I was!"

It was an interesting point of pride for both of us. For her, because she had been hired on her merits. For me, because she had turned out to be the kind of person for whom that meant so much. She had also turned out to be anything *but* "a thankless child."

This is the note I received when she first moved back to New York:

Dear Mom,

So here I am on a plane, descending into Newark. I am completely terrified of screwing up my new job . . . but for all my anxiety, I can only guess that it must pale when compared to your move to NY. I think I'm stressed with movers, a new apartment, etc. . . . . I can't conceive of adding two children to support and an overnight shift to the mix. When I think about what you did, and how effortless you made it seem, I can't help but think I'm the luckiest kid in the world. It's not hard to figure out how I've gotten to where I have. Thanks for everything up to this point, and in advance for the support you'll have to provide when I start calling in tears.

I love you,
Kristen

I called *her* in tears first, to thank her for this incredible gift. As I would with Kerry when she, too, sent such notes, including one that arrived shortly after that missive from Kristen. Kerry had already moved to San Francisco for graduate studies in art and photography, and she figured, accurately, that I was having a bout of the empty-nest blues.

I know that things are difficult with Kristen moving and everything, but I love you and I am just a forty-five-minute plane ride away. Please call if you need support or if you just want to cry. I love you and I couldn't be a prouder daughter.

Love,

Kerry

For any single parent who might be struggling through the early years, take comfort in the knowledge that one day, you, too, may receive such notes, and that *they will sometimes even be devoid of requests for money!*

This is not to say that Kristen and I have moved past our competitive relationship. If anything, it intensified. Even though we talk on the phone several times a week, these conversations always include some variation of the same ritual.

"Mom, I really need to find a good story to pitch."

"Kristen, if I had a story good enough for *60 Minutes,* I sure as hell wouldn't be giving it to you."

Or: "Can't talk now, Mom, I'm heading out to the airport."

"Oh? Where are you going?"

A pause as she considers whether I'll be tipped off by what she says.

"Canada."

A pause as I ponder whether to once again ask the question she has never answered.

"Oh? And what's happening there?"

"Can't talk about it. Gotta go."

This conversation is virtually the same when she asks where I'm heading and why. It is our own version of *Waiting for Godot,* a futile exercise in which each person continues to hope for an improbable breakthrough and is continually frustrated. And yet it's comforting in its sameness. We each need to ask. We each need to refuse to answer.

I am sure there will come a day when she won't even need to ask for the occasional bit of advice. But she still calls now and then, saying something along the lines of, "I need to ask a Journalism 101 question." I love those discussions, always couched in generalities, of course, to avoid giving away the exact details of the story, but usually involving some pithy ethical dilemma, the kind that crop up so often at a high-pressure magazine show but which fewer and fewer people seem to care about. Perhaps it's grandiose to think my concerns in this area will be carried on by my daughter. Perhaps I am even deluding myself. But again, who better to delude me?

The first time I saw her name flash by (in don't-blink-record-time) as a credit on *60 Minutes II,* I was amazed at my reaction. I had expected to be proud, but nothing like this. It took me back to the kids' first dance recital, when they were dressed in hideous bumblebee tutus, with antennae on their little blond heads, and Kerry (then four) could only seem to "pirouette" in one direction and Kristen (then five) could only seem to "pirouette" in the other direction and the two of them so disrupted the "flight" of the bumblebee lineup that the whole audience of stage mothers was soon abuzz at the debacle. The same sense of perverse pride that had reduced me, back then, to tears of both laughter and love washed over me again as I saw my daughter's name whisk by before my eyes. Now this, I thought. What next?

I doubt that I will ever get over that sense of pride as I watch my kid's name on a *60 Minutes* broadcast. At the same time, it is bittersweet, this semi-passing of the baton. It's an odd relay race in which the handoff runner slaps the baton into the waiting palm of the more refreshed runner and then refuses to actually *let go.* And so we run in lock-step, at least for now.

This was brought home to me in a recent conversation. Kristen called to ask if I had seen her piece the night before. "Oh God, honey, I forgot your piece was airing last night. I missed it!"

"But Mom, I *told* you."

"You told me, but *last week.* I need to be reminded on the same day. I forget things. Don't take it personally."

"Well, I'll send you a tape."

"Thanks, and I'm sorry. By the way, did you see my piece last night on *Nightline?*"

"I didn't know it was going to be on last night."

"I know I told you."

"I'm sorry, guess I forgot."

"I'll send you a tape."

It's a comfort to know that even our slights are in sync.

Kerry, meanwhile, is relieved to be free of this competitive drama. She thrives in a world of art and design (yes, including her own tattoo), none of which she gets from me. This frees me up to be constantly amazed at her talent without the underlying edge of competition. Sometimes it is something simple, like the day she came home for a visit, took one look at my new sofa, and said, "No, no, no, *no!*" And by shifting the damn thing fifteen degrees to a diagonal position, she transformed the whole room. I'd been staring at it for weeks, but hadn't really *seen* it.

I also try never to shop without her. She moves through a store with the aplomb of a senior buyer for Saks, whipping outfits off the racks, and *mirabile dictu,* finding just the right *accessories* to go with them. Once, she picked out, yes, a *scarf* for me and said, "Wear this, Mom. It will make that suit come alive."

I wasn't sure I wanted my suit to come alive, and said so, but realized I was being defensive. There it was, that scarf thing again. Perhaps the consultant wasn't so far off the mark, after all. But it would take someone I really trust, like a daughter with a great eye, to convince me to buy one. She even taught me how to tie it with flair, a skill I promptly forgot after she went back home to San Francisco.

"I never see you wearing that scarf on television, Mom."

"Oh, I will, I will." I lie, too embarrassed to admit that I can't tie a simple scarf without looking as though I had a date with the hangman.

She is now polishing her skills as a photographer, which are considerable, prompting me once to suggest, ever so delicately, that she might consider a career as a photojournalist. She gave me that "good try" look.

"I'm not interested in that stuff, Mom. That's you and Kristen. I'm interested in artistic shots, faces, interiors, landscapes."

"Photojournalists can do all that," I pushed on.

"But they have to go to dangerous places to do it. Who needs it?"

She is excellent yin to my yang.

As for my partner in yang, the race goes on. I got a call recently from my friend Mike Graham, a screenwriter who used to be a Detroit cop and who has excellent police sources and story ideas. I've picked his brain on any number of occasions for stories I've done for *World News* and *Nightline.*

"I'm faxing something to you," he said.

"What is it?"

"It's a fax I received from your daughter. Thought you'd get a kick out of it."

"Why would you be getting a fax from my daughter?"

"Well, we've been exchanging some information. I asked her for a videotape of a piece *60 Minutes* did on Colombia."

Here is what her fax said: "Hey Mike! Here's a copy of our show. Enjoy! . . . If you have any good stories to share, remember: My Mom would rather have you help me, a struggling upstart pounding the dirty New York City streets, than giving her yet another *Nightline* ☺. Best, Kristen Muller."

I can't decide what was harder to take, that smiley face or Mike's cover page, which said, "Judy, this kid bears close watching!"

Yes, she does, bless her little cutthroat heart. And yet, I still melt when she calls with a frantic question.

"Mom!"

"Yes?"

"Do you know the country code for Burma?"

"No, I don't. But how hard could it be to look it up?"

"Not hard." Big sigh. "I just thought you might know. And I missed you."

"I miss you too, honey." Slight pause. "So, what's happening in Burma?"

CHAPTER

12

———

NOW THIS

The barn has burned down.
Now I see the moon

—ZEN SAYING

A few barn-burnings, cougar-pouncings and Skaggit-skirmishes later, I have arrived at a fascinating place, a place called To Hell With It. This is no way implies cynicism or defeat; in fact, it is just the opposite. It is, quite simply, *perspective,* an understanding that *very few things* are worth getting worked up about because almost *all things* pass. This includes felonious nannies, uppity adolescents, satanic squirrels, dates from hell, earthquakes, and yes, even O. J. Simpson.

This is not to say, of course, that I have achieved such a high level of consciousness (nowthisnowthisnowthis) that I can deal serenely with every bump in the road at the moment it is happening and promptly "let it go," as we say in California. No, this is to say that, given enough *time,* I can usually see what an idiot I've been to take such stuff seriously in the first place, and given even *more* time, get over it.

And so, in the moment, some of those bumps still throw me. Like the time I was berated over the wording of a script by an executive producer for *World News Tonight,* a woman who has since found employment elsewhere. But at that particular time, she was employed as my boss and, when it came to editorial differences of opinion, represented a sizable bump in the road. Or pothole, perhaps, since you could rarely see it coming.

I had written a closing piece for our show about singer Pat Boone's decision to do something of a comic turn in a heavy metal outfit, all leather and chains and fake tattoos, much to the consternation of the folks at the Christian television network, who failed to get the joke and promptly canceled Boone's evangelical program. Despite the fact that Boone had chosen the rock classic "Stairway to Heaven" as one of his debut songs in this genre (a rendition that could not have been more milquetoast if it were dipped in treacle), his Christian bosses felt he was doing the work of Lucifer and had to be stopped.

You can see why this would make such a delicious story to tell, especially since Boone said he had learned an important lesson in how painful it is to be discriminated against based on the way you dress, and vowed to be more tolerant of punk rockers and others of their ilk in the future. It was pure Moliere, *Tartuffe Takes a Holiday*. And the initial response to the script I submitted to the Rim was enthusiastic. "Just one thing," said the editor going over my script. "The executive producer would like you to condense that last paragraph, make it a little bit tighter." Then he proceeded to dictate the wording she had suggested.

My mistake, apparently, was in thinking her wording *was* a suggestion. I rewrote the last paragraph into a shorter version, using my own words, edited that version, and sent it in. After it aired on the East Coast, the phone rang. It was this same executive producer, calling *from the control room*. She was so furious, she couldn't even wait to return to her office. There was no "hello," no greeting of any kind.

"I thought we told you to change that last paragraph!" she shrieked.

"But I *did!*" I was stunned at the virulence of her attack.

"Don't tell me you did. I asked you to remove that word and you purposely ignored my instructions!"

"What word?"

"The word 'well'!"

"Well?"

"It's a cliché! It says 'look at me, the correspondent, I'm so clever!' "

"Well," I said (and for some perverse reason, I could not stop saying it for the duration of this conversation), "I didn't get that message. I was told to condense that paragraph. Besides, 'well' sets up the listener's ear for a bit of irony to follow. It can be, well, a very effective device."

"Don't tell me you didn't know! I specifically gave instructions on how that paragraph should read!"

"Well . . ." I started to say in reply, but she had hung up.

Despite the fact that she later wrote an email, apologizing for her outburst and saying how much she liked the piece as a whole, I found myself obsessing about the number of times other correspondents used "well" in their scripts, with no repercussions. This is not an inspirational example of "letting go." Within three months, I had collected a number of examples, almost all of them written and delivered effectively. I knew it had gotten out of hand (shades of the squirrels!), when I would leap up in the middle of the broadcast, and shout, *"There's another one! Did you hear it? Aaron Brown just said "well!"*

Since no one in the newsroom knew what the hell I was talking about, these moments of righteous satisfaction would be extremely short-lived, downright hollow, in fact, and I soon gave it up. But until the day that producer left the network, I could not stop saying "well" in just about every conversation we had. It was more than a Freudian slip. It was a Freudian assault.

The war over "well" definitely fits into the category of Small Stuff, as in: what you shouldn't sweat. And there's nothing like some Big Stuff to remind you of that. In April of '99, that lesson was delivered with a vengeance, when I covered a story that tapped into almost every life experience I had had up to that time, and drew on every bit of my emotional strength.

I first got the word in a message on my pager. I was in Newport Beach at the time, interviewing some teenagers with eating disorders, for a *Good Morning America* story. "Shooting in Denver," said the readout on my pager. "Leave for airport now, then call buro."

It was extremely unusual to dump out of a two-camera shoot that had been planned for so long, involving so many people. I knew it had to be important. We made our apologies and our exits almost simultaneously. Once in my car, I called in to learn that I was to head for the John Wayne Airport in Orange County where we had chartered a jet to take me, a producer and a crew to Colorado. The shooting, I was told, was at a high school in a suburb called Littleton, and it was still "in progress." No word yet of any fatalities, but it didn't look good.

This had the feeling of a long-term assignment and I realized I had no change of clothes (I now always carry a packed bag in

my trunk). I was wearing sandals, an innocent enough decision
that morning in California but a huge mistake two days later
when a freak spring storm brought snow to Denver. These things
may seem trivial, but when you're slogging through snow, and
then through mud, it certainly adds to the jumble of uncomfortable sensations associated with such a story.

Actually, "uncomfortable" doesn't begin to describe it. "Emo-
tionally wrenching" comes only slightly closer. When I arrived
at the scene, I couldn't get near the school, which was still surrounded by SWAT teams. We knew that there were at least two
gunmen, reportedly high school kids, and that there were numerous casualties. No one had yet used the word "fatality." My
crew and I went to a nearby library, where parents were waiting
for word on what had happened to their kids. It was a chaotic
scene, since many students who fled the school had run to nearby
homes of friends, and parents simply had to wait to find out if
they were all right or if they were still inside Columbine High
School. Red Cross officials at the library were regularly listing
names of kids who called into a hotline that had been established.
The list was updated every half hour and posted on the outside
of the building.

I arrived just as the list was being posted for perhaps the
fourth time. I watched the expressions on the faces of those parents as they pressed forward, searching for the names of their
children on the list, names that would tell them, yes, it will be all
right, none of this is real, she's going to walk through that door
tonight just like she always does.

And at that moment, I was not a reporter. I was a parent. I
could no more have walked up to one of those people, who
clearly were experiencing one of the worst moments of their

lives, and ask them a question than I could have driven a knife into my own heart. Which is about how I felt, at least empathically, as I watched one woman searching in vain for the name she needed so desperately to see, then realizing, no, it's not there, how could it not be there, it must be there, looking again, frantic now, then falling into the arms of her husband, sobbing, her husband trying to reassure her, no, no, there's still time, we don't know anything, it's early yet, she'll call in, you'll see.

Our camera crews stood back from the scene, filming quietly and from a distance. But I know how hard it was for them to film at all. They, too, were parents.

And yet, we had to do our jobs, to tell the story to a nation that waited, horrified, for the facts of yet another school shooting, one that would prove to be the worst ever, the one that would once again prompt cries of *no more,* but louder and more insistent than ever before.

My colleague Tom Foreman, who lived in the area, found the story especially difficult, not just because he, too, is a parent, but because he had friends in this school system. He had been pulled from another assignment, as well (he'd been ready to board a plane to Macedonia), and was covering the Littleton shooting for *World News Tonight.* On that first day, I was covering for *Nightline.* I decided to write the piece as a timeline, especially since we could not guess at the outcome, or whether we would have all the salient facts by air time. So I began by shooting a standup at the library, citing the time and noting what was happening there. I stood as far from the crowd of parents and students as I could, so as not to appear insensitive, but it still felt that way. Just to *be* a reporter at that place and time was an anguishing experience. Our very presence felt like an affront.

I struck up a conversation with a woman who was standing off by herself. She was a teacher at Columbine, she said, an English teacher who had hustled her kids out of the school upon hearing that shooting was going on. And so I found myself in yet another moment of empathy, this time imagining myself trying to be brave before my students, trying to lead them to safety, the whole time wondering if any of us would be targets. This conversation also triggered a long-repressed memory of one my students back at Metuchen High who had committed suicide, with all its haunting, unanswerable questions of could-I-have-done-more and why-didn't-I-see-it. And I knew the teachers at Columbine would be asking themselves the same haunting questions in the days to come.

Even as I empathized as teacher and mother, I *identified* myself as a reporter and somehow found the courage to ask her if she could talk to me, on camera, about what she had seen. She frowned, looked down at the ground, and then surprised me by agreeing to do the interview. This would not be the last time that week that I would be surprised by the willingness of people to share their experiences, almost in a mass wave of catharsis, unfailingly polite in their responses. It somehow made the asking even tougher; a slammed door in the face is something you would expect in this instance, something you almost feel you deserve. I wondered if I would slam the door, under the same circumstances. I thought I probably would.

We somehow got on the air that first night (actually, we always get on the air, a feat that never fails to strike me as miraculous), and it was not until I got to my hotel room that I broke down. So many dead, so many wounded, such a waste, and worst of all, the terrible *sameness* of the story, the now-familiar how-can-it-happen-here to where-did-we-go-wrong to what-can-we-do-to-stop-it-next-time to the inevitable, clichéd search for *closure,* surely the ultimate obscenity in light of the enormity of *this* school shooting, so much worse than ever before, but no, some reporter would no doubt utter the C-word before the week was over, the word that so utterly trivializes and debases grief.

When we drove up to the school parking lot the next morning, my worst fears of media excess were realized; there, sprouting like overturned toadstools in the mud, satellite dishes pointing at the sky as far as the eye could see, part of a media encampment that was growing by the hour. Surely, I thought, we can find a better way.

And in the middle of all that, an impromptu memorial park had sprung up, starting with bouquets at the abandoned car of one of the victims. By week's end, this memorial would take on a life of its own, spreading tentacles of flowers and balloons and poems and pictures up and over the hill, attracting hordes of mourners with nowhere else to take their communal grief.

I remember a lot about that week, but the quote I remember the best came from a woman visiting that memorial. She said, "What's really sad is that we already know what to bring." Such memorials had become institutionalized, from Oklahoma City to Springfield, Oregon, to all the other cities where madness had erupted, prompting yet another round of, "But we never thought it could happen here."

That first morning after the shooting, producer Peter Imber and I were assigned to do a profile of the victims. It was a reporter's worst nightmare: asking impossibly intrusive questions in order to get seemingly impossible answers, aimed at summing up a life in a matter of seconds, and all this against terrible deadline pressure. Since there had been no official word yet on who the victims were, we started the day with a feeling of dread. First we had to find out who they were; then we had to ask someone, a family member or friend, what they were like.

We knew an African-American boy was among the dead seniors, so we got hold of a yearbook. This school was so overwhelmingly white, that it didn't take us long to figure out his name. As Peter drove our rental car through Littleton, I sat in the passenger seat, flipping through the phone book. I found the name, dialed the number, and listened as it rang. Each step of the way, I was torn between hoping I would fail in this endeavor and worrying about that deadline ticking ever nearer.

A man answered and said, yes, he was the boy's father. He did not hang up on me, which surprised me because *I* would certainly have hung up on me. I said we were wondering if we could talk to him very briefly about his son.

His son, I was thinking, his son who never came home yesterday, his son who would never come home again, and here we are, the media monsters come to ask him how he feels about that. I wanted to get sick.

"Well," he said slowly, "that's all right with me. But did you say you're with ABC?"

"Yes."

"Well, I'm a little confused. ABC is already here. Do you want to talk to them?"

A producer from *20/20* got on the phone and asked me what I was doing.

"I'm doing a story for *World News,*" I responded, "and we just need a brief interview."

"Well, that's not going to be possible. *Dateline* is setting up in the next room and we're talking to him right after that."

So this is what it had come to. Magazine shows were no longer just vying with broadcasts from rival networks, they were vying with broadcasts from their own networks. I told her I would only take a little bit of the father's time, and that I was almost at the house. Then I hung up.

We were about a block away, when the cell phone rang. It was the New York desk, calling us off. "*20/20* has agreed to give you a couple of soundbites after the interview," said the editor. "They just feel it will be disruptive if you show up."

I wondered if *20/20* would have made that offer if I had not pushed it. They certainly had not shared the information ahead of time. But I did agree on one thing: the fewer the better. In fact, I so hated this task that I wondered if we couldn't find a better way to cover these stories in the future, perhaps pooling our efforts to the point where no family would be requested to speak more than once. But this would require cooperation among hundreds of media outlets, all of them with a tradition of competition, not cooperation. And even though this idea pops up after each of these shooting incidents, it is quickly forgotten as those media outlets weigh anchors and sail away to other troubled waters.

By the end of that second day, meaning deadline time, we had assembled enough material to report on the teacher and students who had died. "To the rest of the world, they are victims," I wrote, "but to their families and friends, they are much, much more." I was trying to say, up front, that we knew our words would be inadequate. I knew that to be true—as a storyteller, as a teacher, and as a parent.

For me, the story of the Columbine shooting was an intersection of all my experiences, and it took place in a city that reverberated with echoes of my past. Driving from the scene of the story to my hotel every day, I passed all the emotional landmarks. There was the condominium where I struggled to support my kids after my divorce; there was the motel where I stayed when I returned for the custody battle; there was the courthouse where I came so close to losing my children.

And here I was, talking to people who had lost theirs forever.

Perspective. It broadens and deepens the story, at the same time that it makes you realize you really have no control over where that story will go. One day you're talking to teenagers in Newport Beach who are worried about losing weight and the next day you're talking to teenagers in Littleton who are worried about losing their lives.

As I watch these stories unfold, and try to tell them in a way that will connect with the lives of those who have pulled up the proverbial chair to listen, I am repeatedly struck by the calming effect of giving content to chaos in the form of a story, and the healing effect of sharing that story, whether it's around a campfire, in a room of recovering alcoholics, or in millions of living rooms connected by images bouncing off satellites orbiting an ever-smaller planet. Communal stories that are both calming and humbling, because despite our best efforts to "wrap it up" in a nice tight package, reality is messy and happy endings elude us.

My mother used to say, "I just hope I live long enough to see you happy." She didn't, at least not by her definition, which I came to understand meant a happy *marriage*. This Cinderella myth is a dangerous one on a number of levels, telling us everything will be hunky-dory *just as soon as he* comes along, or *the job* comes along, or, in perpetuation of the myth itself, *the kids grow up to be happy*.

It is a terribly seductive lie, this just-as-soon-as equation, this curse of happily ever after, and it calls to us in our loneliest moments. Even though experience tells me that offering up my heart one more time can lead to terrible pain, the impulse to connect with someone else, to share my stories with his, to write new ones together, is a powerful force. The trick is never, ever, to assume you can dictate the ending—to *anything*.

Happiness is the "Big Get." It is the elusive exclusive that will rocket you to fame and fortune. And it is a fiction. I am continually amazed, instead, at the power of the "Little Gets," the moments in the here-and-now that make up the rich stuff of life, not to mention the best material for a story. But I've been steeped in the Happiness Myth, so "consciousness" takes practice. And yet, being fully conscious of the Little Gets, both the pleasurable and painful variety, is its own reward. To connect with a strange woman reading a list of strange names in a strange town with such an emotional intensity that you can barely stand it is to be fully conscious. It is not the stuff of headlines. It is the stuff of the heart.

And in hindsight, I can see that every "setback," from divorce to derailed career opportunities, has provided a jump forward. If someone had said so at the time, however, it would have annoyed me no end. I still believed I could impose my own script on this unfolding story. Now I know I am more of an audience than I ever realized, and that the most control I can hope for is a little selective editing now and then.

And if I get ahead of myself, there's always that old radio cue to fall back on, that simple mantra to remind me that the only moment that counts is *this* one, right *now.*

It would also make one hell of an epitaph.